KINGFIZZER

Kingshuk Nag studied at the Delhi School of Economics and worked at Tata Economic Consultancy Services, the Associated Chambers of Commerce and Industry of India (Assocham) and *Business India* before joining the *Times of India* as its first business news chief in New Delhi. Subsequently, he was its business editor (south) in Bangalore and resident editor in Ahmedabad and Hyderabad. Presently, he is the editor-in-chief of KhabarStreet.com, an online news portal he has launched.

Winner of the prestigious Prem Bhatia Award for excellence in political reporting and analysis for his coverage of the Gujarat riots of 2002, Nag is the author of several books, including *The Double Life of Ramalinga Raju: The Story of India's Largest Corporate Scam*; *Battleground Telangana: The Chronicle of An Agitation*; *The NaMo Story: A Political Life*; *The Saffron Tide: The Rise of the BJP*; *Atal Bihari Vajpayee: A Man for All Seasons* and *Netaji: Living Dangerously*. His works have been translated into many languages, including Hindi, Bengali, Telugu, Marathi, Kannada and also Mandarin.

KINGFIZZER

The Rise and Fall of Vijay Mallya

KINGSHUK NAG

HARPER
BUSINESS

First published in India in 2017 by Harper Business
An imprint of HarperCollins *Publishers* India

Copyright © Kingshuk Nag 2017

P-ISBN: 978-93-5264-287-8
E-ISBN: 978-93-5264-288-5

2 4 6 8 10 9 7 5 3 1

Kingshuk Nag asserts the moral right
to be identified as the author of this work.

HarperCollins *Publishers*
A-75, Sector 57, Noida, Uttar Pradesh 201301, India
1 London Bridge Street, London, SE1 9GF, United Kingdom
Hazelton Lanes, 55 Avenue Road, Suite 2900, Toronto, Ontario M5R 3L2
and 1995 Markham Road, Scarborough, Ontario M1B 5M8, Canada
25 Ryde Road, Pymble, Sydney, NSW 2073, Australia
195 Broadway, New York, NY 10007, USA

Typeset in 11.5/15.5 Sabon LT Std by
R. Ajith Kumar

Printed and bound at
Gopsons Papers Ltd

For
Dr Chiranjib Kumar Basu (Khokhan dadu),
who gifted his portable Hermes typewriter to me
on learning that his college-going grandnephew
had become a freelancer for newspapers

Contents

Mallya's Businesses at a Glance

1955: Vijay Mallya is born on 18 December to Vittal Mallya and Lalitha Ramaiah

1974: Appointed director on the board of United Breweries

1983: Inherits Vittal Mallya's businesses (liquor, beer, food products, pharmaceuticals, agro chemicals, paints) with an estimated annual turnover of Rs 350 crore on his death

1983 onwards: Begins ramping up Kingfisher beer

1985: Failed attempt to manufacture and sell EPABX systems

1985-86: Abortive bid to take over Shaw Wallace

Late 1980s: Starts and abandons pizza and cola-like drink businesses; starts UB Air, a private air taxi service

1988: Starts Kingfisher Derby

1988-90: Acquires engineering firms Best & Crompton and Western India Enterprises

1990: Acquires Mangalore Chemicals and Fertilizers

1991: Sells Berger Paints that he had inherited

1992: Takes over Kunigal Stud Farm started by Tipu Sultan two hundred years ago

1994: Plans for light rail transit systems for Bangalore

1995: Consolidates all liquor businesses into two companies (McDowell and Herbertsons); failed bid to brand West Windies cricket team as Kingfisher West Indies team; plans to enter mining, hotels

1996: Enters newspaper publishing

1998: United Breweries buys 50 per cent equity of Mohun Bagan and East Bengal; Mohammedan Sporting rejects bid

2000: Gets into making customized software

2000 onwards: Kingfisher beer becomes an internationally recognizable brand

2000-04: Acquisition of domestic breweries and distillers

2004: Work on UB City, billed to be Bangalore's biggest commercial property, begins

2005: Kingfisher Airlines becomes airborne; acquisition of Shaw Wallace (including its brand Royal Challenge)

2006: Forms United Spirits by consolidating all his liquor businesses (Shaw Wallace, McDowell, Herbertsons, Triumph Distillers)

2007: Acquisition of Whyte & Mackay, Scotland-based Scotch manufacturing company; acquires Deccan Aviation, which operated Air Deccan

2008: Kingfisher merged into Deccan Aviation; gets into F1 motor racing; becomes franchisee for IPL team called Royal Challengers Bangalore

2009: Heineken buys equity in United Breweries and becomes equal partner; loan of Rs 950 crore from IDBI Bank for Kingfisher Airlines

2010: McDowell Signature Indian Derby starts with prize money of $400,000; luxury residential complex Kingfisher Towers planned; Kingfisher hit by engine maintenance problems; Kingfisher debts restructured by banks after accumulated debts top Rs 7,000 crore; Kingfisher international flights stopped

2012: Kingfisher Airlines is grounded

2013: Diageo takes over United Spirits

2014: Mallya loses Mangalore Chemicals and Fertilizers; Karnataka High Court restrains UB (Holdings) from selling flats in Kingfisher Towers

2015: SBI tags Mallya, Kingfisher Airlines and UB (Holdings) as wilful defaulters; CBI begins probing the loan by IDBI Bank to Kingfisher Airlines

2016: PNB follows suit and tags Mallya as wilful defaulter; Mallya is convicted in a cheque-bouncing case; non-bailable warrant issued against Mallya and he is declared a proclaimed offender; the stage is set for Heineken's takeover of United Breweries

2017: Extradition proceedings against Mallya begin; he is arrested by the Scotland Yard on 18 April after the Indian government sends a request for extradition, but is granted provisional bail within hours on a bail bond of £650,000 and the condition that he would remain at the address provided by him.

Preface

INDIA CHANGED SLOWLY BUT surely after the economic reforms of July 1991 began the process of liberalization. The reforms opened up the economy, bringing in opportunities for Indian entrepreneurs who were willing to modernize and upgrade their capabilities and face competition from foreign players. The laggards were destined to perish as they could not adjust to the changing times, used as they were to operating in a sheltered environment. In a few years, changes to the industrial and business landscape of India gathered pace, and many old, established players started to fall by the wayside even as new ones emerged.

One of the early movers who leapt on the liberalization bandwagon was Vijay Mallya. Having inherited a readymade drinks empire in 1983 after his father's sudden demise, he realized that he would have to face competition from foreign players, who sooner or later would show up on the country's shores. Following the dictum 'Join them if you cannot beat them', Mallya started forging alliances with foreign liquor majors to strengthen his empire while also diversifying his own. Over the next decade and a half, he went a step further, becoming owner of production facilities and companies abroad. His non-resident Indian (NRI) status helped him run both his international and domestic businesses with ease, something he had realized in the late 1980s after his failed attempt at buying the blue-chip Shaw Wallace. His business acquired a global facet. At the same time, he was accumulating all kinds of personal assets, such as luxury houses and vintage cars, quickly gaining the reputation of being an open-fisted spendthrift. He was also known to be fond of the company of women, and the liquor king's opulent lifestyle in the fast lane was much talked about.

Mallya was also considered to be cocky and arrogant. In fact, he was almost everything his father was not. The senior Mallya, an enormously rich man, was almost a miser who lived an austere life poring over balance sheets. He kept severely to himself, and few beyond his intimate circle knew him. He was barely recognizable in public.

One of the most important changes brought in by liberalization was in the politics of the day. This has not been adequately recognized, leave alone studied, but it gave impetus to the rise of costly politics by bringing more money into elections. It also brought businessmen into politics. Until then, businessmen had restricted themselves to financing elections and taking favours from politicians elected to office. But now, with more money to spare, they began to enter electoral politics. Here was a direct route to getting business: why give money to politicians and then wait for them to get elected to be granted favours? A more effective way was to get elected as public representatives and use the newfound clout to get things done directly.

Mallya too realized that being a politician was not a bad deal, and in 2002 powered his way into the Rajya Sabha, getting elected again in 2010. Each time he used a different political party, displaying his clout across the board. In between, he also led a political party that contested elections across Karnataka but failed to make an impact.

Success soon went to Mallya's head. He sought to launch an airline under the brand name of Kingfisher, riding high on the success of his Kingfisher beer, by then a globally known brand. The airline would be of a different kind from the run-of-the-mill ones, and would offer the choicest of food, luxury and entertainment. But he lost sight of the fact that running an airline globally was a highly risky business and that more airlines were going down than soaring high. Moreover, in a country like India with a middle class still only graduating to air travel, the key to success lay in low fares. A low-cost, no-frills airline was the formula to success.

It was with the launch of Kingfisher Airlines that all of Mallya's troubles started. But the 'king of good times' (as he loved to be called) was late in realizing this. He wanted to expand his business to fly overseas. So he acquired the older, low-cost Deccan Aviation (which ran Air Deccan flights) and merged it with Kingfisher for a better experience record, a prerequisite for a licence to fly abroad. His troubles began to mount by 2008-09 as a result of the global downturn and rising prices of aviation fuel. Here, his contacts came to help. He was able to persuade a consortium of banks to lend him a huge sum of money and restructure his earlier loans. But the downslide that had begun could not be stemmed and, in fact, matters became worse. In 2012, the airline sank, leaving behind unpaid staff and creditors. Mallya, always surrounded by his admirers, probably did not see the end coming and till the last looked for more money to somehow flog to life his grounded airline. His friends put forward the argument that the government of the day had gone out of its way to promote rival airline Indigo and support the sinking state-owned Air India. But no money came his way.

His lifestyle was his addiction. Although his airline sank, he continued to live the fine life. He had expanded his activities and had taken over football teams, like Kolkata's Mohun Bagan and East Bengal, and had established an IPL cricket team for Bangalore, Royal Challengers Bangalore. He had to ultimately sell off the liquor empire he had assiduously nurtured from the fledgling it was when his father left it in his care. Diageo, the largest liquor company in the world, is now the new owner of United Spirits. Much of his beer business (United Breweries) is also gone: it is only a matter of time before Heineken shuts him out of the beer empire he himself built.

The allegations by the Central Bureau of Investigation (CBI) and the Enforcement Directorate (ED) make out that Mallya began diverting cash from his own company from 2010, stashing away part of it overseas. This was to fund his lifestyle abroad and to invest in activities like F1 racing, goes the claim. The impression is that he was doing this even as his companies were going to seed and bank loans remained unpaid. In the end, the banks—which took a rather soft approach towards him to begin with—had to declare him a wilful defaulter. He was now officially someone who had the wherewithal to repay his loans but was not doing so. His sixtieth birthday celebrations in December 2015, where he was said to have burned away crores of rupees, was the ultimate cue that set the banks after him. Now, enforcement agencies are listing his assets abroad.

Getting wind of his imminent arrest, Mallya fled India and is now living in the UK. He has evaded many summons from investigating agencies. His Indian passport has been revoked. He has been declared a proclaimed offender by Indian courts and now extradition proceedings have been initiated against him in the UK.

On 14 June 2017, the ED filed the first charge sheet against Mallya in the case of the Rs 900 crore loan from IDBI Bank under the Prevention of Money Laundering Act (PMLA). The 5,000-page charge sheet also named five officials of IDBI Bank and two executives of Kingfisher Airlines. It accused Mallya of entering into a criminal conspiracy with the other accused to secure the loan. He was also accused of diverting a large part of the loan for his personal expenses and to the entities owned by him.

His is a tale of our times—a heady cocktail of power politics, women and money; a tale of a bright young man whom luck favoured with an inheritance on whose foundations he built a huge empire, only to see it crash like a house of cards as he overreached.

June 2017
Hyderabad

1

The Beginning of the End

AS THE CLOCK STRUCK midnight on 18 December 2015, two sets of fireworks rent the night air at Candolim and Sinquerim beaches in Goa; they were so loud they could be heard in Panaji 18 km away, startling the locals. The fireworks went on for a full five minutes without a break. Tourists still ambling on the beaches took out their phones and cameras to capture the display.

The occasion was the sixtieth birthday of the 'King of Good Times', Vijay Mallya.

Mallya was already deep in hot water, the banks having declared him a wilful defaulter, but this in no way diminished the grandeur and scale of the celebrations for his landmark birthday at his home in Kingfisher Villa on the Goa beachfront.

In attendance were 200 friends and well-wishers who had flown in from every corner of India and all parts of the globe, and were staying at the nearby Taj Holiday Village and Taj Fort Aguada. The guests were treated to a two-hour non-stop session of Bollywood numbers by Sonu Nigam, who concluded it with '*Tum jiyo hazaron saal, saal ke din ho pachas hazar'*. But the chief attraction of the evening was the king of Latin pop, international icon Enrique Iglesias, who had travelled across the globe to sing for Mallya. He belted out his 2014 chart-topper *'Bailando'* to say happy birthday as Mallya's son Siddharth touched his father's feet on stage, seeking his blessings.

The grapevine had it that $2 million was spent on the party, described as 'the mother of all bashes'. Even as the extravagant party was in full swing, Kingfisher Villa had a sword dangling over it; its takeover by the lenders whom Mallya had defaulted had been permitted by the Goa bench of the Bombay High Court. This was to be the last of Mallya's many, many high-end events at the villa.

The party drew adverse comments from many quarters, among them Raghuram Rajan, then governor of the Reserve Bank of India, who said in a characteristic understatement: 'If you flaunt your birthday bashes while owing the system a lot of money, it does seem to the public that you don't care. I think this is the wrong message to send. If you are in trouble you should be cutting down your expenses.' Rajan did not name Mallya in this statement reported in the *Times of India* on 23 January 2016, but everybody understood whom he was referring to.

The staff of the grounded Kingfisher Airlines also expressed their disgust. 'He (Mallya) does not have money to pay our dues. How can he have such gala bashes and be insensitive to our sufferings?' they complained, even as it surfaced that some of Mallya's close associates had cautioned him against such a lavish affair. They had advised him to limit the celebrations to a party in London, where he maintained a home. He would then be far away from prying eyes in India, where not only banks but also investigating agencies were on his trail. But these words of caution fell on deaf ears. Mallya couldn't care less about what people said.

Mallya, who appeared to live from party to party, had always celebrated his birthdays in grand style, although the years since Kingfisher Airlines got into trouble had been marked by low-key events. In 2013, there had been an exclusive do at Niladri, his residence off Napean Sea Road, an upmarket locality in Mumbai. Some of his birthday bashes had been on *Indian Empress*, the superyacht he owned.

His fiftieth birthday celebrations—at the same spot in Goa as his sixtieth—had also happened in immoderate style, having been an all-night affair, with the American singer Lionel Richie entertaining guests who had been ferried from all over by two Kingfisher Airlines planes requisitioned just for the party. The invite sent out by Mallya said: 'When I turned 40 a decade ago, I was fortunate to have joined by my closest friends over a three-day celebration that included themed events. While I cross another milestone, I am planning on an exciting but somewhat chilled out series of rendezvous with the Sun, sand and sea in Goa.' Top industrialists, Bollywood stars, politicians and an assorted assemblage of the wealthy and the fashionable had turned up.

———

Less than two-and-a-half months after his sixtieth birthday, Mallya spirited himself out of India and away from the reach of the long arm of the law. The rumour in New Delhi was that he had been tipped off by a mandarin that he could be soon behind bars as legal proceedings against him were imminent. The tip was not passed on to Mallya directly; it was said a high-profile fixer-cum-socialite obtained this information from the mandarin and passed it on to Mallya, who lost no time in making his exit. Mallya had also come to know that on 28 February 2016, senior Supreme Court counsel Dushyant Dave had advised the State Bank of India to approach the courts to restrain Mallya from leaving the country. The SBI took its time to act, but Mallya did not.

On 2 March 2016, Mallya, holding a diplomatic passport—by virtue of his being a Member of Parliament—whizzed through immigration with ease and boarded the London-bound Jet Airways flight 9W-122 from New Delhi. According to newspaper reports, Mallya occupied seat 1D in first class and was accompanied by a lady who was later identified as his current girlfriend, Pinky Lalwani, once a hostess on Kingfisher Airlines. Mallya had carried seven pieces of luggage, indicating that this was no short business trip. Usually this quantity would account for the luggage of at least five passengers.

At the airport, Jet Airways staff loaded Mallya's luggage while he retired to the premium plaza lounge. It appeared that Mallya had spent an hour in the lounge. News reports said he walked slowly—very slowly—out of the lounge, and that the immigration officials noticed his exit but did not do anything to prevent him from boarding his flight. They had no orders to detain him or to prevent his exit. The reports also said Mallya's tickets had been booked only hours in advance (the same day in the afternoon), giving credence to the theory that he left post-haste after learning that danger was at his heels.

A lookout notice for Mallya had been issued by the Central

Bureau of Investigation (CBI) to the Bureau of Immigration on 16 October 2015. This would have led to his detention the moment he presented himself at any immigration counter. Now, a lookout notice is usually not revised, but Mallya, besides being an MP, had top contacts; this may explain how the notice was amended barely a month later, on 24 November 2015. The amended notice required the immigration authorities to merely inform the CBI about his movements; it did not authorize them to detain him. It is interesting too that he had arrived in India from an overseas trip on the night of 24 November, a few hours after the CBI had amended its lookout notice.

Earlier on the same day that he finally fled India, Mallya had been spotted in the lobby of Rajya Sabha, of which he was member. Nobody who met him there had any clue that he would soon make his escape out of the country.

A couple of hours after Mallya was well airborne, then CBI Director Anil Sinha lambasted the chiefs of India's top banks, including the SBI chairman, for not filing complaints against him in good time, telling them how their tardiness had delayed action against the liquor baron. At the annual session of the Indian Banking Association, the CBI chief would remind the bankers that his agency had to file cases suo motu against Mallya in the absence of first information reports initiated by banks.

Sinha was quite unaware for some time that the liquor baron had flown away for good, as Mallya had been frequently flying in and out of the country in the recent past. He had flown out on 1 December 2015 and had returned on December 7; he had flown out again on 23 December and returned on 2 February 2016. His last overseas trip before his escape to London was to Barbados in the West Indies, where he was negotiating the purchase of a cricket team for the Caribbean T20 cricket league. During this visit he also met with the prime minister of Barbados, Freundel Stuart, in the end bagging the Barbados Tridents. Rather misleadingly, Mallya later claimed that he had paid just $100 to win the team. But realizing that nobody would be fooled by this claim, he said later that the cost of running the team for a season would be $2 million. He also claimed that he had bought the team in a joint venture and the Barbados government would give him subsidies to run the franchise. 'They are keen to help,' he said.

It was only on 9 March 2016 that the news of Mallya's escape became public when the Attorney General of India Mukul Rohatgi informed the Supreme Court about it. All hell broke loose. Questions were asked about how Mallya had escaped in spite of a lookout notice against him, and the CBI was forced to clarify that it had downgraded its advisory to the immigration authorities because the case against Mallya was at a preliminary stage and there was no clinching evidence against him other than that he had reneged on repayments to banks. The CBI also said that lookout detention orders were usually made against individuals for whom there were non-bailable warrants. There was none against Mallya. That he had flown out of the country many times and had returned was evidence that he would not abscond and that he would be available for questioning if required in the future, CBI officials argued. Mallya himself tweeted on the same lines on 11 March 2016: 'I am an international businessman. I have to travel to and from India frequently. I did not flee from India and neither I am an absconder. Rubbish.'

The CBI was proved wrong. On 25 February, less than a week before he fled the country, Mallya had got a huge severance package from United Spirits Limited (USL). This was a company that he had built but had subsequently lost control of after the Kingfisher Airlines fiasco. The company had been taken over by the world's largest liquor manufacturer, Diageo Plc., in 2013. But since USL was a company that Mallya had built from 1983—when he took charge of it after the demise of his father—he had an emotional connect with it. Diageo thought it fit to allow Vijay Mallya to continue as chairman of the company. Although Diageo had done its due diligence on USL before taking it over, the Indian company still had much else to reveal, which Diageo discovered only after taking control of it. Alarmed by what it saw, Diageo commissioned a special audit of the books of accounts of USL, only to be confronted with the fact that Mallya had transferred Rs 1,225 crore from the company to entities that he privately controlled. Immediately the new management of USL asked him to step down. At first he refused but later agreed—on the condition that he would be paid a severance package, of which US$40 million would be paid upfront and the rest in tranches over five years.

Mallya scooted as soon as he got the money. During the run-up to this, the CBI had no clue about what was going on. If the agency had well-informed sources, it could have filed a criminal complaint against Mallya for making away with cash from USL and arrested him as he attempted to board a flight out of the country. The CBI, however, did have some clue that Mallya had allegedly pilfered cash from the company because it was around the same time that it made a reference of the matter to the Enforcement

Directorate (ED), which looks after violation of provisions of the PMLA.

Though the Diageo-controlled USL informed the bourses about the findings of its audit and also disclosed details of the deal to get Mallya off its back, it informed them about the money transaction with him only after the cash had been paid. Consequently, a stay on this payment by the Bangalore bench of the Debt Recovery Tribunal (DRT) on 7 March 2016 was infructuous, and banks looking for recovery of their cash from him were left high and dry. It was again on 7 March that the ED filed cases of money laundering against him; around the same time the SBI approached the Supreme Court to block his exit from India by cancelling his passport. But he had already fled the country, a fact that had to be then disclosed before the Supreme Court.

Safely ensconced in the United Kingdom, Mallya released a statement on 6 March that gave the impression that he was still in India. The statement accused the media of starting a witch-hunt against him. He asserted that he would always be available to investigating agencies. He pointed out that he was an NRI and had been one for twenty-eight years, implying that flying in and out of India was routine for him. 'I have no intent or reason for absconding,' he said. He claimed that there was no evidence of his wrongdoing in Kingfisher and that 'Kingfisher was launched on the basis of a viable business plan vetted by SBI Capital Markets and renowned international aviation experts but despite every effort it was an unfortunate commercial failure caused by macro-economic factors and then government policies.'

He also hinted that he was being targeted: 'None of these

large borrowers, whose debts are significantly more than the Kingfisher debt, have been declared as wilful detractors but UB (Holdings) and I have been declared so on technical grounds.' It is true that Mallya is not the only example of a corporate chieftain reneging on repayment of bank loans. But, at the same time, none of the chieftains of these other companies so uninhibitedly lives the opulent life. Mallya's open display of his grand life has been the reason why he has attracted so much negative attention.

Mallya may protest his innocence, but going by the sequence of events it appeared that the fear of being nailed on the alleged money laundering charges and consequent arrest made him fly out of India. The unfolding of subsequent events suggests that he has no intention to return.

After landing in London, he seemes to have headed directly to the massive Hertfordshire mansion that he had bought from racing driver Lewis Hamilton's father. Anthony Hamilton had sold the house near Welwyn Garden City to Mallya in July 2015 for £11.5 million. The mansion—named Ladywalk—sits on an estate of 30 acres on Queen Hoo Road in the village of Tiwen. It is heavily barricaded and allows Mallya the kind of privacy not possible in his London home. That home is located on Baker Street in central London, just two houses away from Madame Tussauds museum. (221b Baker Street is the address of Arthur Conan Doyle's fictional detective Sherlock Holmes and a museum now stands there.) Just as Mallya had anticipated, a horde of television crews headed to Hertfordshire as soon as news of his having left for London broke in India. He remained incommunicado but the prying newshounds were able to figure out that he had had many visitors on the previous days, that he frequented a local pub often and was locally well recognized.

————

Predictably, Mallya's disappearance raised temperatures in India, including in Parliament. Finance Minister Arun Jaitley maintained that there was no arrest order against Mallya and that the CBI had moved the courts for cancellation of his passport after he had left. But the Opposition Congress was strident. Leader of the Opposition in the Rajya Sabha Ghulam Nabi Azad alleged that Mallya had been allowed to escape by the government. 'The government is a party to this conspiracy and the Supreme Court should take note of this,' he thundered. Parliamentary Affairs Minister Rajiv Pratap Rudy said Mallya 'is no saint for us', and not 'a single penny was given to him by the NDA (National Democratic Alliance) government', alluding to the fact that Mallya was a beneficiary of the largesse given by banks during the time of the previous Congress-led United Progressive Alliance (UPA) government.

The parliamentary duels apart, both the man on the street and business analysts believe that Mallya, with his wide-ranging contacts across political parties and the bureaucracy, had managed to bamboozle the system and make good his escape. As columnist Kenneth Rapora wrote in the international business magazine *Forbes*, 'Mallya's escape hatch is making mockery of Indian justice and the ruling BJP. Finance minister Arun Jaitley defended Mallya's departure saying that the banks had not initiated the legal process for leaving the country by the time he boarded the flight out of India. How convenient. The ex-Forbes billionaire may be bad at running an airline but has hunch for timing legal matters perfectly.'

The first arrest warrant against Mallya was made more than a month and a half after he disappeared. On 18 April 2016, a special court issued a non-bailable warrant against him in response to a petition filed by the ED, which accused him of siphoning off Rs 430 crore from an IDBI Bank loan to Kingfisher Airlines to purchase properties. The ED had sought the warrant after Mallya skipped three summons issued to him to appear before the agency—on 18 March, 2 April and 9 April. Mallya had written to the agency that he would not be available before May because he was negotiating the repayment of his loans to commercial banks through the intervention of the Supreme Court. 'This was a very specious agreement because return of loan cannot be linked with probe for breaking the law. Even if he returned the loan, the liability for transgressing the law is not obviated,' Supreme Court advocate Diljeet Singh Ahluwalia says.

Vijay Mallya's name has since figured in the Panama papers that were released by the International Consortium of Investigating Journalists. The *Times of India* reported in its 9 April 2016 edition that Venture Net Holdings Ltd, registered in the British Virgin Islands and operating since 15 February 2016, was linked directly to Vijay Mallya (and not to one of his companies). Venture Net has an offshore link with Particullus Trust, which is a one-stop solution for setting up offshore accounts and is registered in Cook Islands in the South Pacific.

Incidentally, the Supreme Court had also directed Mallya

to appear before it on 30 March 2016 with his passport. Predictably, Mallya did not show up. The Supreme Court came into the picture when a consortium of banks led by the SBI approached it after realizing that Mallya had been able to circumvent the DRT. The court subsequently asked Mallya to give it a list of properties that he owned 'in a sealed cover'. After much dilly-dallying and arguing that this would compromise his and his family's privacy, he did provide a list, but one that was incomplete.

In order to pressure him to appear before them, the ED requested the foreign ministry to revoke his passport in the fond hope that such a move would force the liquor baron to scurry back home. As a first step, the foreign ministry suspended his passport on 15 April, asking him to explain why it should not be revoked. Later, the passport was cancelled. But this did not serve the objective of getting Mallya home from London because under the Immigration Act 1971, 'the UK does not require an individual to hold a valid passport in order to remain in the country'. Her Majesty's government officially told the Indian government: 'We can't deport Vijay Mallya over an invalid passport. Consider requesting mutual legal assistance or extradition.'

Mallya's extradition is theoretically possible using the extradition treaty signed by the two countries in 1993 and a Mutual Legal Assistance Treaty (MLAT) signed in 1992. However, in practice, extradition is not an easy process because it requires approval from courts in the UK after their hearing of charges and the defence. Merely because the law-enforcing agencies want Mallya back in India does not mean that courts in the UK will be sympathetic to the demand. 'If Mallya hires good lawyers, as he is bound to, the process will become complicated and more delayed,' Supreme Court lawyer Diljeet Singh says.

Only one Indian, Samir Patel, wanted for the post-Godhra violence, has been extradited by the UK since the treaty was signed. Hopes for Mallya's extradition were raised after British Prime Minister Theresa May's visit to India in November 2016. Indian Prime Minister Narendra Modi presented to her a list of sixty people wanted in India and currently ensconced in Great Britain. The list included Vijay Mallya. May promised all help, and the Indian government has now invoked the MLAT. A visit by Jaitley to London has also raised hopes. But top officials in the Government of India are sceptical about Mallya's extradition from the UK so easily. Mallya was arrested by the Scotland Yard on 18 April 2017 after the Indian government sent a request for extradition. But, as per the norm, he was granted a provisional bail within hours of the arrest on a bail bond of £650,000 and the condition that he would remain at the address provided by him. Moreover, he has to be in touch with the authorities and his mobile phone has to be accessible all the time. But he remained cocky and tweeted: 'Surrender of passport, arrest, bail, all part of normal extradition proceedings.'

There is every indication that he will argue before the courts in the UK that he is being singled out for victimization. This is clear from his tweets. Arraigned by the ethics committee of the Rajya Sabha—the custodian of moral and ethical conduct of its members—Mallya sent out a series of messages. 'In all humility and not in defiance as they report, I would like the Indian media to check and verify facts before calling me a defaulter,' he tweeted in April 2016. Another tweet said: '7686 defaulters owe PSU banks Rs 66,190 crores.

It is easy to blame only Mallya.' In yet another he declared: 'The allegations against me are blatantly false. I am shocked that the Finance Ministry has provided factually wrong information to the Parliamentary Committee.'

But the Rajya Sabha ethics committee, headed by the veteran Karan Singh, remained unconvinced by his defence. On 25 April 2016 it decided to recommend termination of his Rajya Sabha membership. Having got wind of this a little earlier, he post-haste faxed a resignation letter to Rajya Sabha Chairman Hamid Ansari. But it was rejected because the letter did not follow prescribed procedures and did not carry Mallya's original signature.

Considering that his membership was coming to an end on 30 June 2016, its termination in early May made little difference to his Rajya Sabha tenure. But to be officially kicked out of the Rajya Sabha was for Mallya a slap in the face.

That he had decided not to return to India was made clear by his lawyer's argument in the Supreme Court as early as 26 April 2016. His lawyer said: 'He has no intention of coming to India soon because he is sure to be clapped in prison given the recent actions against him. If he is arrested the moment he comes in and taken to Tihar jail, it serves no purpose.' The lawyer was arguing in the context of the repayment of the bank loans taken by Mallya. He seemed to be apprehensive that he would meet the same fate as Subrata Roy of Sahara. Roy, who partnered Mallya in the Formula One team for some time, had been sent to New Delhi's Tihar jail in February 2014 on the orders of the Supreme Court. The court had given him interim bail, which would be operative only if he paid up Rs 10,000 crore to the capital market regulator, the Securities and Exchange Board of India (SEBI). Roy would have had to sell some of his assets to generate that money but failed to do so.

Almost five months after his escape, Mallya, through his lawyer, sang a different tune. Failing to appear before a Delhi lower court for non-appearance in a Foreign Exchange Management Act (FEMA) case, he sent an email that was presented to the court. He said he was unable to come down because his passport had been revoked and that he was trying hard to get the passport cancellation revoked. The case relates to the alleged payment of $200,000 to a British firm, Benetton Formula, to advertise Mallya's company's liquor products at the Formula One World Championship in London.

Attorney General Mukul Rohatgi, however, asserted in court that Mallya was a fugitive from justice and was playing 'hide and seek', and cooking up 'cock and bull stories'. He alleged that Mallya was 'deliberately concealing something from the banks', and also seemed to be of the view that he had 'no intention to come back'. Mallya, on his part, has said in a *Financial Times* interview on 29 April 2016—his first after his flight from India—that by cancelling his passport and arresting him, the Indian government cannot expect to get any money.

As the law took its slow course, Mallya appeared fully devoted to enjoying himself in the UK. In late May 2016, his son Siddharth posted a video that showed the father-and-son duo watching the Indian Premier League (IPL) final in London on TV. In the video Mallya is seen rooting for Royal Challengers Bangalore, a team he had established. Siddharth also mentions Force India's third place in the Monaco Grand Prix finals. Mallya continues to hold equity in Force India. Mid-June 2016 saw Mallya at the elite Ascot races, where only thoroughbred horses compete.

On 18 June, Mallya was spotted at the book release function of *Mantras of Success: India's Greatest CEOs Tell You How to Win,* co-authored by Suhel Seth, who was Mallya's junior at school. The event at the South Asia Centre of the London School of Economics also had Indian High Commissioner Navtej Sarna in attendance. Sarna, who was a co-panellist at the event, walked out on spotting Mallya among the gathering. Later, the organizers of the function said that Mallya had not been invited but had come because admission was open to all. Mallya expressed deep offence, saying he was not a gate-crasher and could not be one, and was at the function because the author was his friend.

While enjoying the good life in London, Mallya is also making his case by continually broadcasting his innocence. In an interview to *Auto Sport,* carried in its July 2016 edition, Mallya insisted that he was being subjected to a witch-hunt, noting that he could not go to India because his passport had been cancelled. He said that if Indian authorities wanted to interview him, they could come to London, talk to him on radio link or send him an emailed questionnaire. 'I will reply. I have nothing to hide,' he stressed. 'I am not physically present in India and they issue an arrest warrant and cancel my passport. What confidence does that give me on their real intent?'

In mid-June 2016, Mallya was declared a 'proclaimed offender' by a special court in Mumbai, empowering the ED to seize his properties. This was a squeeze of sorts for Mallya but was not enough to smoke him out of Great Britain.

In February 2017, India invoked the MLAT and asked Great Britain to extradite Mallya on the basis of a non-bailable warrant for arrest issued against him for using bank loans given to Kingfisher Airlines to buy properties. India's request to Interpol for an international red corner notice has also not yet been processed; apparently, Interpol wants more information to be sure that such a notice can be granted. For the record, Interpol is yet to accede to India's request to issue a red corner notice for Lalit Modi, the former IPL commissioner, in spite of the request having been made many years ago.

Given his situation, it is not impossible that Mallya may have acquired a passport from a third country or is trying to acquire one, ran one conjecture. This would give him protection from Indian authorities, but an Interpol red corner notice—if one is issued—will jeopardize his movements. Many think that Mallya will try for British citizenship, says Supreme Court criminal lawyer Diljeet Singh Ahluwalia. He has properties in the UK and has been staying there regularly for long periods. In fact, his NRI status has helped him stay there. Those in the know of things say that the UK is the perfect haven for somebody like Vijay Mallya. He has multiple homes there and has a chance to restart his liquor business there too if he wants to. One of the terms of his disengagement with United Spirits was a non-compete agreement he had to sign with the company, pledging that he will not enter into a competing business anywhere in the world except the UK.

Moreover, the UK gives refuge to all sorts of individuals, and experts say that if Mallya can convince the authorities there that his life and liberty are in danger in India, he can well obtain asylum there on the grounds of human rights. Lawyers specializing in immigration matters say that the UK is a safer haven than even the US for people like Mallya. He can even have a robust family life there. He had once remarked that having turned sixty, he would now like to spend more time with his children and less on business. All his children—a son and three daughters—live abroad. His only son, Siddharth, who has even quit his board seat at UB Holdings, wants to be an actor and train overseas for it.

In his home country, the court cases against Mallya continue to pile up. After he left for London, he was convicted by a Hyderabad court in a cheque-bouncing case filed by GMR Hyderabad airport. The cheques had been issued as payment for services availed at the airport by Kingfisher Airlines. However, a warrant issued by the court cannot be served to him as his address is unknown. On 6 August 2016, a Delhi court too issued non-bailable warrants against him in a similar complaint filed by the Delhi airport authorities.

————

Many are sceptical that Mallya can ever be brought back to India, much less to justice. Although the Indian government may have initiated extradition proceedings, it is not going to be smooth sailing because the British justice system does not allow for easy extraditions. 'The laws are tough, and the only Indian sent back did not oppose the extradition proceedings. Moreover, with Indian agencies like the ED having already seized Mallya's assets, his lawyers will argue that the value of the assets is more than what he owes the banks. So, is somebody making him the poster boy of default? Is this a case of political vendetta?' says Ahluwalia.

Mallya could also use his powerful public relations machinery to change the discourse about him. Media reports are currently focused on his great escape and the fact that he diverted his company wealth into personal investments abroad, but an effort could be made to project the picture that Mallya actually wants to pay up his debts and that nobody is interested in working out a deal with him. The banks are demanding Rs 9,000 crore from him. Mallya is disputing this figure, saying he took loans of no more than Rs 6,000 crore. The interest payment on that and the interest on the interest that has not been paid have added up to make it Rs 9,000 crore. Mallya could argue that due to commercial failures, he made huge losses and cannot pay the entire amount and that banks should take the principal and settle the matter. He can say that the banks and the government are not interested in this solution but want to punish him instead. If this sob story goes around, public opinion about him can change, though he may still be hard pressed to explain his exorbitant lifestyle. Many analysts, however, feel that such a change of image is not possible for Mallya because 'he is ever ready to shoot off his mouth'.

The Government of India is very keen to get Mallya back and prosecute him. This is because of Prime Minister Modi's resolve to punish all black money generators and economic offenders. But many tracking the Mallya affair feel that the government should have shown the resolve from the very beginning and ensured that he did not leave the country. The resolve is coming midway through the case,' says the chairman of a private bank. The government now proposes a new law to confiscate properties of fugitive economic offenders who abscond from India to defy the legal process.

Most Indians believe nothing very adverse will happen to Mallya because nothing ever happens to corporate fraudsters in the country. A good example is the case of the information technology giant Satyam that went bust after its promoter Ramalinga Raju confessed to having cooked the books at his company. Raju was arrested and put on trial. In the end he was handed a sentence of seven years' imprisonment. But within a week of incarceration he got bail and is now living in his home! He is now said to be running a new business through his son and daughter-in-law. There could be an encore of sorts in the case of Vijay Mallya! Like Raju who lost Satyam, Mallya has lost United Spirits and could well lose United Breweries where he is still the chairman, but whose majority shareholding has passed on to Heineken, which is the co-promoter.

Mallya will have his liberty although he cannot venture into India. He will become a truly non-resident Indian who does not reside in India. What the staffers of Kingfisher Airlines wrote to him in an open letter in March 2016 will then ring true: 'People like you start a company with our money, exploit the system and wind up operations without an iota of shame.'

2

Kingfisher Airlines: The Take-off and the Crash

AS CHIEF OF CORPORATE communications at the UB group, Sunita Budhiraja had once sought an appointment with Vijay Mallya. After very many requests to meet him, she was finally given time with the boss. They were to meet at a downtown five-star hotel in Bangalore. That meeting in early 2005 is still vividly etched in her memory. Sunita arrived at the appointed time at the hotel, but Mallya was busy and took his own time coming. He was interviewing and checking out candidates who had applied for the job of cabin attendant (read air hostess) for Kingfisher Airlines, which was yet to be launched. As part of the interview, the candidates were made to walk the ramp.

'It seemed that Mr Mallya was selecting beauty queens,' Sunita recalls. The mood in the UB group was upbeat. 'We, as loyal employees, were very proud that our boss was on the way to setting up a top-class airline. We felt very happy.'

The airline was finally launched on 9 May 2005. The inaugural flight was from Mumbai to Bangalore. Mallya was on board, personally taking care of the guests. They included Civil Aviation Minister Praful Patel and Air India Chairman and Managing Director V. Thulasidas. It was apparent that the airline would be Mallya's favourite baby and he would take all the decisions himself. The previous night there had been a gala at a top hotel in Mumbai, with the who's who of the city in attendance, from top political honchos to Bollywood stars. Mallya was at his ecstatic best: 'We are set to conquer the Indian skies. I offer you Kingfisher Airlines. Come, fly the good times with us,' he had roared.

It was clear to everybody that Mallya was not starting an airline merely to enter the transportation industry. For him the airline also had a glamour quotient; he was entering the business of hospitality. This is something he had made plain to his core team. He had also told them: 'Go and create a great airline brand. Resources won't be a constraint.'

Establishing an airline became a serious aspiration for him around the turn of the century. By then he had well consolidated his position in the spirits and beer industry. He wanted to add more feathers to his corporate cap. In the mid-1980s, he had created an outfit called UB Air, his intention being to enter the airline business the moment the industry was opened up to private operators. This was after the central government in 1986 allowed private players to operate air taxis.

Mallya was very busy with the liquor business when the government did open up the skies. UB Air took up chartered flights for private companies and individuals who could afford them, but business did not pick up, what with the promoter being too busy to nurture it.

His close associates say he was highly influenced by British entrepreneur Richard Branson, a first-generation businessman who, after making money in music, decided to diversify into the airline business. Branson was a showman, the kind who made his own rules. He set up the airline Virgin Atlantic in 1984, challenging British Airways that then ruled the roost in the UK. In the same way Mallya, who even started sporting a Branson-like hairstyle—drawing instant comparisons between himself and Branson—wanted to challenge Jet Airways that had begun to rule the Indian skies (while the state-owned Indian Airlines bled incessantly).

For the record, Mallya never confided to his close aides that he wanted to do what Branson did, but when he first disclosed his desire to enter the airline business, his confidants called for caution. They said the spirits and beer business was doing fantastically well but a safer bet for diversification would be mobile telephony. Being a booming business, this was where money could be made. They pointed out that worldwide the airline business was tough; scores of airlines had gone bust even in the Mecca of free enterprise, the US. In India itself, most of the private airlines that were started in the wake of liberalization—East West Airlines, NEPC Airlines, Damania Airlines and ModiLuft—had collapsed.

But Mallya would hear nothing of this. The aides knew that with their boss's penchant for the good life, he would want to enter the lifestyle business. Mobile could make money, but it would have none of the zing that an airline could bring to his corporate stable. And yes, he would make money from the airline too. In the UB group, he was the boss, and the core team knew that they could argue only this far and no more. He decided the airline would be named Kingfisher, after the group's highly successful beer that had become a global brand by then. Naming the airline after the successful beer would attract the aspirational crowd that India had spawned, courtesy the process of liberalization that had begun in 1991. Scores of mobile upper middle class Indians in the metros scouring for the best things in life would also patronize the proposed new airline. 'The USP of Kingfisher was glamour. "Fly Kingfisher" meant that a passenger was entering the Kingfisher world, one full of parties and great-looking, wealthy folk. So it was aspirational,' recollects R. Krishnan, former aviation correspondent with the *Hindustan Times* and later consulting editor at *Cruising Heights*.

Mallya reckoned that the only competition to Kingfisher would be Jet Airways, an airline that had started operations in 1994 and was among the first to take advantage of the open skies policy announced by the government. In 1994 the Air Corporation Act that had nationalized the airline business in 1953 was repealed, allowing the private sector to operate scheduled services. But Jet promoter Naresh Goyal, although a shrewd businessman who knew how to get things done, had after all had his beginnings as a travel agent and a manager for foreign airlines. Mallya was confident that he would beat Goyal hollow. Events were to prove Mallya wrong.

Kingfisher Airlines was registered in 2003 as a fully owned subsidiary of United Breweries. It took two years to plan the flight path of the airline. Mallya's desire was to do the inaugural flight on Siddharth's birthday as a gift to his heir.

In his zest for the high-flying life, Mallya overlooked many realities. He forgot that the industry preference was for low-cost carriers whose fares would be affordable to the average Indian. Affordability would increase the number of passengers, increasing the size of the pie for all operators. Even at that time most Indians preferred to take the train; air fares were still daunting.

Though he overlooked these ground realties, Mallya was otherwise meticulous as he set about creating Kingfisher Airlines. He asked his team to study 6,000 frequent flyers and gauge their consumer behaviour. Leaving nothing to chance, he wanted his men to go out and personally interview these frequent flyers. Needless to add, he wanted to poach flyers from Jet Airways and the J-class passengers from Air India. To this end he was liberal with upgrade vouchers.

Passengers, many curious to check out the new airline, reported that the flight attendants were pretty and the food and in-flight entertainment good. Since liquor was not allowed on the domestic sector, Kingfisher offered it to first-class passengers in the airport lounge. On take-off, every Kingfisher flight played a video recording of Mallya exhorting his passengers to have a good time and thanking them for flying Kingfisher. 'It felt nice to hear the airline promoter saying that "he respected your business" and thanking the passengers for choosing Kingfisher when he had other airline options as well,' says Deepak Gambhir, a businessman for whom Kingfisher became the preferred choice. What also warmed the hearts of Kingfisher travellers was the announcement by Mallya that he had told his crew to treat passengers as guests at his home. A video showed model and actor Yana Gupta demonstrating to passengers the use of the seat buckle and other safety procedures. Every Kingfisher seat, even on the domestic sector, had a dedicated in-flight entertainment service. 'Dr Mallya had requisitioned the services of top designers Prasad Bidappa and Manoviraj Khosla to design the uniforms of his air hostesses, and he himself was involved in the process, down to details like the material that would be used,' says Sunita Budhiraja.

'It seemed that Mallya was creating the Air India of yore when J.R.D. Tata was in charge. Mr Tata used to take personal interest in the flying crew and their grooming because he wanted to use Air India as another arm of Indian diplomacy abroad,' says Jitender Bhargava, who was director at Air India when Kingfisher started operations. But there was a difference—Air India flew abroad, whereas Kingfisher flew domestically.

Very soon, Mallya's desires became only too apparent. He too wanted to fly overseas. However, for Indian carriers to qualify to fly the international sector, the Directorate General of Civil Aviation (DGCA) norms required five years of flying experience on their part.

With his hometown Bangalore emerging as the Silicon Valley of India, Mallya wanted Kingfisher to fly direct from the city to the original Silicon Valley (San Francisco). He also wanted to fly to London from Bangalore. With this in mind, he made a bid for Subrata Roy's Sahara Airlines when it was on the block in 2006. But Jet Airways too wanted to acquire Sahara. Naresh Goyal had read the market signals correctly and knew that a low-cost arm would only increase Jet's passenger base. Ultimately, Goyal pipped Mallya, although the Kingfisher boss's entry into the fray increased his cost of acquisition. Sahara was then converted into Jet Lite, the low-cost arm of Jet.

Scouting around for an alternative, Mallya realized that there was one airline literally in his backyard. Air Deccan was started in 2003 by Captain G.R. Gopinath, who was also from Bangalore. Gopinath had envisaged Deccan as a low-cost carrier that would connect metros with second-tier cities in India. It would be the common man's airline; its tagline was 'Simply Fly', signifying how it was possible for the common man to fly. Its first flight on 23 August 2003 was from Bangalore to Hubli. Deccan became the first low-cost carrier in India.

Although the market for low-cost carriers was expanding rapidly, running such an airline was still not a profitable business. Gopinath thought that if his scale of operations could be increased, there was hope of his company making profits. On 25 January 2006, Air Deccan had filed a red herring prospectus with SEBI, announcing that it wanted to raise money through an initial public offering. A red herring prospectus is issued by companies when they first raise money on the stock market. It is basically a statement of intent that the company wants to go public. Many details, such as the financials and even the number of shares to be offered, are often not supplied in the prospectus. These are filled in later, close to the time of the issue. In the event, Deccan offered 25 per cent of its shares to the public. The IPO barely managed to scrape through, even though it was kept open for an extended period. This was not surprising because the airline was bleeding. It had reported losses of Rs 340 crore ($74 million) for the fifteen-month period between 1 April 2005 and 30 June 2006.

By now, Gopinath knew how uphill his task would be. So when Mallya approached him to sell out, he was not disinclined. Gopinath figured out that Mallya was desperate, so he struck a good bargain. However, when Mallya first publicly announced that he would take over Air Deccan, Gopinath's response was quite derisive. Mallya's announcement had come at a press conference at the Delhi airport hangar, where a $300-million super jumbo jet A380 had flown in directly from Airbus's manufacturing facilities in Toulouse, France. The plane had been ordered for Kingfisher. When correspondents sought a response from Gopinath, he said: 'We are from different planets. He is from Venus, I am from Mars. We are from opposite ends of the business spectrum, consumer models and consumer space. We are from the bottom of the pyramid, he is picking the cream from the top. The two can't coexist. One airline will kill the other.' This was, of course, what happened in the end.

But the merger did go through and was announced on 19 December 2007. Mallya picked up a 26 per cent stake in Deccan for Rs 550 crore. Gopinath was left with 17 per cent of the shares; market sources said his profit from the sale was in the region of Rs 200 crore.

It was on the basis of Deccan's five-year flying history that Mallya wanted to seek permission to fly overseas. To this end, it was Kingfisher that was merged into Deccan Aviation. The merger was effective April 2008, following which Deccan Aviation was renamed as Kingfisher Airlines! Mallya became the chairman of the company and Captain Gopinath the vice-chairman. The combined fleet of the two airlines was sizeable: seventy-one Airbus A320s and ATRs that flew sixty-nine Indian cities and operated 537 flights.

The greater synergy resulting from a large common fleet was expected to yield good financial prospects for both the carriers under the merged entity.

By September 2008 Kingfisher had started flying overseas. The first flight was to London. True to Mallya's promise, the first class on long-haul Kingfisher flights was a sheer delight. The first class had flat beds with only an 18-degree incline, a seat pitch of 78 inches and seat width of 20–24.4 inches. Passengers were given Merino wool blankets, Salvatore Ferragamo toiletry kits and pyjamas to change into. There were five-course meals and alcoholic beverages on board, and an air hostess made the bed. There was also a break-out area to boot, and a chef on board.

In the early days of the merger, Mallya retained the Deccan identity of a low-cost carrier. He added the tagline of 'Simplifly Deccan: The Choice is Simple'. But the original colours of the airline were changed to the red of Kingfisher. A few months later, this service was rechristened Kingfisher Red. But Mallya's heart was not in low-cost services. Captain Gopinath now believed Mallya had a 'step-motherly' attitude to the acquired airline. Gopinath was quoted in a *Business Standard* interview on 2 October 2011 as saying: '…low-cost aviation was being treated as a step-child. I was telling Mallya that it was now his child and there should be equal treatment. Post the merger if there was an Air Deccan flight and Kingfisher flight at the same time slots, a decision was taken to do away with the Air Deccan flight in the hope that the passengers would graduate to Kingfisher full service. But the opposite happened, the passengers went to other low-cost carriers.'

Senior journalist R. Jagannathan, writing in FirstPost on 1 April 2014, pointed out the inherent contradiction in what

Mallya was trying to do. 'When Mallya bought Air Deccan he failed to see that running a low-cost carrier is different for a full service airline. He made the mistake of calling it Kingfisher Red and reduced his full service brand to the level of a cut-price carrier despite much higher costs.'

Jagannathan noted that running an airline successfully required continual cost cutting, 'but Mallya ratcheted up his costs wherever he could—whether it was handing earphones to passengers or costly gourmet meals in the business class'.

An employee of the airline says: 'There were no cost controls and there was a lot of wastage and pilfering. You could walk into Crawford Market in Mumbai and find on sale cutlery from Kingfisher with the airline markings. A lot of food was also wasted and unused bottles of beverages, instead of being used in a subsequent flight, were just thrown away.' But the experience of travelling overseas on Kingfisher Airlines was great, she recalls. 'You would not be treated so well on your marriage day by your in-laws,' says C. Shankar, a Bangalore-based chartered accountant. 'For offering premium services, a good businessman also charges a premium on his product. But Kingfisher's fares were not any higher than other airlines'. All this was the problem.

On 28 September 2011, Mallya announced that the operations of Kingfisher Red were being terminated because the company did not believe in low-cost services.

'It betrayed that Mallya's business model was wrong. His decision to exit the business was precisely when low-cost airlines like Indigo and SpiceJet were spreading their wings and garnering a huge lot of new flyers,' says Bhargava.

Indigo had commenced operations in mid-2006. The company was a joint venture between Rahul Bhatia, who came from a family in the travel business, and Rakesh Gangwal, an aviation veteran based in the US, who had been earlier chairman and CEO of US Airways. From the beginning, Indigo was focused; it entered the low-cost segment and that was where it stayed. It operated the same type of aircraft and kept operational costs low, emphasizing punctuality (something Indian travellers desperately needed). The airline grew by leaps and bounds, and by December 2010 had replaced Air India (into which Indian Airlines had been merged) to become the third largest airline in the country. It was still behind Jet and Kingfisher, but by the beginning of 2012 it had become the only profitable airline in India. Later, it also replaced Kingfisher to take the second slot.

The first flight of SpiceJet was in late May 2005. The airline was a remodelled, low-cost version of ModiLuft that had ceased operations in 1998. Kalanithi Maran of Chennai had infused a lot of funds into the company post 2008, buying up nearly 39 per cent of its equity. Though the company was making losses, it had significant volumes and was the second largest low-cost carrier in India. 'The promoters of both Indigo and SpiceJet realized what the name of the game was and were successful in their own way. Mallya did not realize, or rather would not recognize, that the future lay in cheaper air tickets,' says journalist Krishnan.

———

Of course, it is wrong to say that Kingfisher was not doling out cheap tickets. The fares offered by Kingfisher on all sectors were competitive; it was lack of cost control that ruined the airline.

Globally, 2008-09 turned out to be a year of reckoning for the aviation industry when a strange phenomenon began to play out. On the one hand, there was a slowdown in both the global and Indian economies and a recession that led to reduced passenger growth rates; on the other, global fuel prices jumped. This was a contradiction because in normal circumstances a slowdown should lead to reduced prices of raw materials, including oil. But the cartel that runs oil prices globally wanted to maximize revenues even as demand fell. So there was a 23 per cent increase in the price of aviation turbine fuel (the increase effected in many tranches) in 2008-09. This immediately affected the operational costs of airlines, and in India this was reflected in higher ticket prices (25-30 per cent higher during the period), which in turn led to a decline in passenger traffic that had been growing strongly in the previous years.

In India, central government imposts and state government levies on petroleum products, including ATF, are high, translating into airlines paying 60–70 per cent more for fuel than in the rest of the world. This broke the backs of the airline companies. The imposts were non-discriminatory and affected all domestic airlines equally; it was not that Kingfisher was affected more adversely than the other airlines. However, operating as it was on a defective revenue model— of high costs and low revenues—Kingfisher crashed faster than it could have been imagined.

Even in the midst of this aviation crisis, the average ticket prices offered by Kingfisher were still moderate compared to those of Jet Airways. Mallya wanted his passengers to continue living the good times. According to an aviation industry study, the average price of a Jet ticket in 2006-

07 was Rs 5,295, against Rs 3,410 for a Kingfisher ticket; and the corresponding figures in 2008-09 were Rs 6,190 and Rs 4,942 respectively. In such circumstances, the gap between operational revenues and costs was widening, both for Kingfisher and Kingfisher Red. In fact, even in 2007-08, Kingfisher's expenses were Rs 3,510 crore, against revenues of Rs 2,890 crore. In the same fiscal year, Kingfisher Red spent Rs 2,810 crore, but could garner revenues of only Rs 1,550 crore. These are operational losses; as the term indicates, they constitute the losses made on running the airline. When the costs incurred on paying interest on borrowed funds and other such expenses are also taken into account, the net losses greatly exceeded operational losses.

More trouble was on the way. In 2010, the airline was hit by a major engine maintenance problem in its A320 fleet. A dozen of its aircraft had to be grounded because the airline had insufficient guarantees in place in its contracts with the engine manufacturers. This led to piling of costs and more losses.

But Mallya betrayed no signs of panic. On the contrary, he appeared cheerful, whether from trying to project sheer bravado or from not realizing the extent of trouble his airline was mired in. His tweet on 28 April 2010 (as reported by *Mint* newspaper) went: 'Ooo la la le o OOO la la la oo la o. someone asked me why I owned a booze company and an airline. I said both make us fly. Cheers.'

Later that year, on 9 October 2010, he stated: 'On a hectic roadshow meeting potential investors in the planned Kingfisher equity raise. Amazing to see smart Indians managing billions. Kingfisher had faced unprecedented difficulties in the past one year but our staff has done a superb job of maintaining quality. One by one each hurdle has been addressed squarely and resolved. Now watch Kingfisher India's only five star airline REALLY fly.'

By this time Kingfisher had gone down irretrievably. But it flew on through the dust and turbulence for some time until it was grounded on 1 October 2012. When it ceased flying, Kingfisher was still serving twenty-five domestic destinations. International flights had stopped a few months earlier; the last flight left London for New Delhi on 10 April 2010. When it was grounded, Kingfisher had sixty-four aircraft, most of them from the Airbus family.

Its last year of operations was especially troublesome. Unable to pay lease rentals, Kingfisher had to return thirty-two of its leased aircraft, which restricted its flight schedules. The airline did not have money to pay for fuel. And, by the time it stopped flying, Kingfisher's debts to the public sector oil companies, from whom it was buying ATF on credit, had swelled to Rs 1,000 crore. Its pilots and other staff were restive because the airline was unable to pay their salaries on time: in fact, the airline was unable to pay their salaries even during the festive season. There were allegations that the company was not even depositing the mandatory employer's provident fund contributions to the authorities.

There were frequent instances of cancelled or delayed Kingfisher flights. In some instances, the bank accounts of the company were frozen. British Airways cancelled its code-sharing agreement with Kingfisher. In February 2012, the DGCA ordered a special audit of Kingfisher Airlines' operations to ensure that its financial problems were not compromising customer safety.

In the years that it flew, the airline never made profits, and in only one year (ending March 2010) did it make operational profits. Though the airline stock was traded on both the National Stock Exchange and Bombay Stock Exchange, it yielded only negative earnings for the shareholders all through. In the period between June 2007 and March 2013, the airline's accumulated operational losses exceeded Rs 6,000 crore and its net losses amounted to nearly Rs 14,000 crore.

————

The saga of a company is different from that of a human being. The relatives of a patient in deep coma put him on life support systems and then are in a quandary as to whether to pull them off or keep the systems going for some more time. But, for a company, cessation of operations is not the end of the story. The entity continues to be in existence with all its assets and liabilities. Before the company can be wound up (which is when the company ceases to be), all its tangible assets have to be sold and the proceeds distributed to those to whom the company owes money. The whole process has to be carried out in accordance with laws that have been laid down for the purpose.

In the case of Kingfisher, despite all its troubles, Vijay Mallya remained quite sanguine. He thought that with the infusion of the right kind of funds, the airline could again fly. He blamed the high cost of fuel, the high cost of funds, the falling rupee and high taxes for the woes of Kingfisher, even as he lobbied for higher foreign equity for the airlines sector. This would allow foreign players to bail him out. He was also looking for a government bailout. He argued that, after all, the government had used budgetary resources of thousands of crores to recapitalize the perpetually loss-making Air India just because it was in the public sector. But there were not many takers for his arguments; most people could see that he was going down the path to disaster because of his own failings. Still, many organizations that had tied up with Kingfisher continued to linger around the descending airline, up to the point where it was crystal clear that its revival was an impossibility. For example, Airbus, with which Kingfisher had booked planes, waited till January 2014 before cancelling the orders. Kingfisher had ordered five A380s and five A350 long-haul jets many years ago. Announcing the cancellation of the orders, John Leahy, global sales chief of Airbus, said: 'Mallya still has an operating certificate and is determined to sell the airline. But even if he does sell the airline, we took the internal decision that he does not need the aeroplanes right now.'

While Mallya persisted with his unrealistic attempts to sell Kingfisher, the company's aircraft were all literally rotting in their parking bays. The *Times of India* reported on 8 April 2013 that most of the fifteen planes leased by Kingfisher may be headed to the scrapyard. The report went on to suggest that the lessors of these aircraft discovered that their planes (Airbuses) were simply in no condition to fly and didn't want them back. Many aircraft were missing so many parts that they could not be brought back into shape. The report described how, during the last few months of its operations, Kingfisher was so strapped for funds that it had to keep taking out parts from its grounded fleet to keep a handful of planes airworthy.

As early as 2009, banks with exposure to Kingfisher began to realize that their loans to the airline were unlikely to be recovered. In banking jargon, the loans had become non-performing assets, or NPAs. Huge amounts had been loaned to Kingfisher as it had made an inordinately large order for aircraft. This included a personal aeroplane for the big man himself; on delivery, this machine was to be lavishly fitted out, containing, among other artefacts, a Picasso original. The plane carried a personal identity: A319-VT-VJM—VJM being an abbreviation for Vijay Mallya.

Mallya's preferred choice of aircraft was the Airbus, and those in the know of things say this was also because of the rapport he struck with fellow Bangalorean Kiran Rao, who had been sent to India as a representative of the company to sell its aircraft. (Mallya's other alternative was to buy aeroplanes from rival Boeing). In this business, aeroplanes are typically booked many years in advance, with the booking amount working out to 1.5 per cent of the cost. Full payment is made on delivery, but in the interim period the buyer (the airline) ties up funds from banks and other financial institutions.

Banks faced with NPAs are nearly always in a bind. The option before them is two-fold: either write off the debts and take the losses in their book or lend more money in the hope that the company will turn profitable later so they can ultimately recover their money. The risk with the latter option is the possibility that even the loans given later can be lost. In other words, banks run a double risk. In the case of Kingfisher Airlines, this is exactly what the banks did: taking what they thought was a calculated risk. In November 2010, the banks, for the first time, restructured Kingfisher's debts. The consortium of lenders led by SBI converted loans of Rs 1,355 crore they had advanced earlier to Kingfisher into equity in the company. Not only this, they bought these shares at a price that was 60 per cent higher than the share price of Kingfisher on the stock exchanges. The banks extended themselves even further and stretched the period of repayment of loans to nine years with a two-year moratorium, cut interest rates and sanctioned fresh loans. It was clear that to get such a deal, Mallya was either still able to charm the banks, or the banks were convinced about Kingfisher's ability to get out of the soup it had got into.

Banks typically advance loans against collateral. Mallya surely did provide them with it. One of them was pledge of the brand Kingfisher to the banks. A brand value of Rs 4,100 crore was arrived at by a private consultant, Grant Thornton LLP India. Mallya had also given the banks a personal guarantee of Rs 248.97 crore, while UB Holdings provided a corporate guarantee of Rs 1,601.43 crore. Kingfisher had also provided a pooled collateral security of Rs 5,238.59 crore, including Kingfisher House in Mumbai, Kingfisher Villa in Goa and hypothecation of helicopters that the company owned.

The new loans did nothing to revive Kingfisher and, as noted earlier, the airline stopped flying in October 2012. In another month's time, lenders like BNP Paribas of France filed a petition in the Karnataka High Court to wind up Kingfisher Airlines and UB (Holdings), the company through which Mallya controlled his other companies. BNP wanted the Rs 146 crore that it was owed. The petition was accepted by the high court after a year, in November 2013, and is still being heard. Over the years, many other lenders have also become party to the winding-up petition. This includes SBI and aircraft lessors and engine makers such as Rolls-Royce and IAE.

As of March 2016, Kingfisher Airlines owed eighteen Indian and other banks Rs 6,939 crore in principal and interest dues. Of this, Rs 1,600 crore was owed to SBI and Rs 800 crore each to IDBI Bank and Punjab National Bank.

In August 2013, perhaps realizing that Vijay Mallya and Kingfisher had taken the bank for a ride in offering the brand as collateral, SBI and some other banks decided to take a relook at the brand value. The new valuation—by a new agency—came up with a figure of Rs 200 crore (down from Rs 4,100 crore in 2010, on the basis of which the banks had given further loans to the airline). Two years later, in September 2015, the brand value of Kingfisher was down to Rs 100 crore.

In November 2015, after a Herculean effort that had to be cleared by the Bombay High Court and the Supreme Court, SBI was able to tag Vijay Mallya, Kingfisher Airlines and United Breweries Holdings as 'wilful defaulters'. Under RBI norms, a person or company is declared a wilful defaulter if he/it meets one of four conditions: his loans are not repaid when he has the capacity to do so; he has not used the loan for the purpose for which it was borrowed and diverts the money elsewhere; he siphons off the funds and money is not available with him in any asset form; and he sells off the assets given as security against loans without informing the lenders.

SBI had contended before the courts that funds were diverted from Kingfisher Airlines to various UB group companies and other firms. SBI made the claim after a forensic audit of Kingfisher Airlines. Mallya denied all allegations. SBI also said that UB (Holdings) had deliberately avoided paying its lenders.

Three months after the SBI action, Punjab National Bank on 16 February 2016 also declared Mallya, Kingfisher Airlines and UB (Holdings) wilful defaulters. Chairman and Managing Director of PNB Usha Ananthasubramanian declared: 'When people have the wherewithal to pay, they must pay,' adding that the bank had gone to the DRT and had sought other legal powers before describing Mallya as a wilful defaulter. The United Bank and UCO Bank had also earlier declared Mallya and Kingfisher Airlines as wilful defaulters.

Many government agencies like the CBI and the ED are on the trail of Vijay Mallya, Kingfisher Airlines, some of its executives, and the UB group. The CBI has already got an FIR registered in the Kingfisher matter and is investigating a case regarding a loan of Rs 800 crore it took from IDBI Bank in 2009. Besides investigating the manner in which the loan was given, the CBI is also investigating whether the loan was used for the purpose for which it was granted. The agency, say newspaper reports, seems to suspect that a substantial chunk of the loan was misused to partly pay off other debts that had accrued to Kingfisher Airlines. Part of the funds was also transferred overseas under false pretexts and stashed away in foreign havens. The ED is also investigating the money laundering angle.

Mallya, before he left India on a diplomatic passport in March 2016, was questioned by the CBI in December 2015. Some key officials of the UB group, like its long-time Chief Financial Officer Ravi Nedungadi and the CFO of Kingfisher Airlines A. Raghunathan are still being investigated by the law enforcement agencies. The CBI has now decided to extend the ambit of its probe to look into a staggering 6,00,000 transactions made by Kingfisher Airlines. It is going to be a long while before the investigations wind up and the Kingfisher saga is finally over.

The collateral damages were many, not least of them the indignities the staff of Kingfisher Airlines had to endure as their company went under. Many were literally left on the roads when the airline closed shop. The *Economic Times* reported on 10 March 2016 that the company still owed salary arrears of Rs 300 crore to 3,000 employees. Some of the staffers started to get income tax notices much after the airline had stopped operations. The allegation was that although the airline had made tax deductions from their salaries, it had not deposited the money with the tax authorities, and the tax sleuths were now demanding the money from the employees.

This was a double whammy for them, as they were not getting their salaries in the first place. The pilots at the company were able to bag jobs in rival airlines, but many of the cabin crew and technicians found it hard to find work. Many of the cabin crew joined the hotel industry and some of them even malls. Newspapers reported cases of technicians who had taken up odd jobs. A news story on a Kingfisher technician who was making a living selling garments sewn by his wife was particularly poignant, while in October 2012 the wife of a Kingfisher employee committed suicide in Delhi as her husband had not been paid his salary for six months.

3

Vittal Mallya: The Reclusive Founding Father

The story goes that after declaring a state of Emergency in the country in 1975, Indira Gandhi sought the names of the richest businessmen in India from her intelligence agencies. She wanted to gauge who had the wherewithal to stand up and oppose her rule, or to fund such opposition. When she saw the list, the prime minister recognized all but one name—Vittal Mallya. Who is he, she is supposed to have enquired. The story may be apocryphal, but serves to press home the point that Vittal Mallya was an extremely low-profile businessman who was severely private. He kept so much to himself that he could pass unrecognized even in a crowd of businessmen.

Socially inactive, Vittal spent most of his time poring over company balance sheets. That was his passion, and that was what made him what he was. But Vittal was not your average *munimji* who only knew balance sheets. He had received his education from top-grade institutions in India, having been to the Doon School and to Presidency College, Calcutta (now

Kolkata). Moreover, he got top grades at college, graduating with honours in mathematics—an indication of his affinity for numbers. At school he had been so precocious academically that Doon twice awarded him double promotion.

Vittal was a Goud Saraswat Brahmin from a place called Bantwal, which is around 30 km from the coastal city of Mangalore in Karnataka. Goud Saraswat Brahmins are known for their industry and entrepreneurship; legend has it that around 3,000 years ago, the community lived on the banks of the river Sarasvati in north-west India. When the river began to dry up they migrated to the Konkan region, settling mostly in Goa. But persecution at the hands of the Portuguese in the sixteenth century saw them flee once again, this time further down the coast to what was then known as Canara. That's how Vittal's family came to settle in Bantwal. Traditionally, the Mallyas were known as Mahalyars, which denotes that they were caretakers of the palaces (*mahals*) of the feudal lords called Prabhus.

One of Vittal's ancestors was Ananth Mallya, who as a boy ran errands for several supply stores, quickly learning the basics of business management and eventually venturing on his own to establish a flourishing trading house. So Vittal could have inherited the entrepreneurial gene from his ancestor. His own father was a doctor in the British Indian army. Bantwal Ganapathi Mallya, who was a Fellow of the Royal College of Surgeons (FRCS), rose to become a lieutenant colonel and had served all across pre-independent India. Vittal was born in 1924 when Ganapathi was serving in Dacca, now Dhaka, the capital of Bangladesh. He was the third son of his parents. Ganapathi's continual postings in cantonment towns affected the education of the young lad.

Being in the British army, he wanted his son to have a liberal, Western education, and so when Doon School was opened in 1935 Vittal was dispatched there. When Vittal passed Senior Cambridge and was ready to go to college, his father was posted in Calcutta. Thus the choice of Presidency College.

Vittal had started analysing balance sheets even while in college, and was also putting money in the stock markets. He did not wish to study further after his graduation, much to the disappointment of his father, who wanted his son to become a *pucca sahib*. But Vittal did take his father's suggestion to travel overseas to get a taste of the world. The original plan was for him to travel to Europe, but the continent was in the throes of World War II. And, strangely, he landed in South America. It was such a long journey to make from India but, among other things, he picked up Spanish while there.

Coming back to India, he teamed up with the Nanda brothers Har Prasad and Yudi, who had started Escorts as an agency in 1944. But this association did not continue for more than a year. He now joined Chunilal T. Mehta and Co., a stock broking firm in Calcutta. It was here that he honed his skills; the story goes that he began investing in shares of the Bengal-based Indian Iron and Steel Company (IISCO) and made a killing. His attention was then drawn to United Breweries (UB). The young Vittal started acquiring shares of the company in 1946, and by 1947 had enough shares in UB to be elected as a director in the company, becoming the first Indian on its board. The English were now leaving India and, in 1948, Vittal, barely twenty-four, replaced R.G.N. Price as the chairman of the company. The managing director continued to be an Englishman who had decided to stay on in India for some more time.

United Breweries had a hoary ancestry going back to 1857, the year of the great Indian revolt. Two breweries, Castle Brewery and Nilgiris Brewery, were set up in the Nilgiris to quench the thirst of British soldiers and planters who stayed in the plantations up the hills. In 1902, another brewery, British Brewery Corporation, was established in Madras (now Chennai) to serve the affluent in that city. Still another outfit, Bangalore Brewery, sprung up in 1885 to serve soldiers in Bangalore and Pune.

On 15 March 1915, a Scotsman, Thomas Leishman, bought up all these breweries and amalgamated them into one company, United Breweries. In the inter-World War years, the breweries increased their capacity, supplying mainly to the British troops. The market for domestic beer increased as the other choice for British consumers in the country was to wait for beer from England. This took about five months to be transported by ship. To ensure that it did not spoil on the journey, extra hops had to be added to this beer, which added to its bitterness.

To make his beer more popular, Leishman used bullock-carts to carry it in large barrels and casks called hogsheads. This allowed him to penetrate the market in those days of bad roads and non-existent transport infrastructure.

Vittal was not a man to rest on his laurels. The acquisition of UB had given him confidence, and now he began to look into the balance sheets of other companies in the same space to buy them up. Three years later, in 1951, he acquired McDowell and Company Limited. This was a firm that manufactured spirits, not beer. McDowell had been established in 1826, again by a Scotsman, Agnes McDowell. In the beginning, the agency was in the business of import and distribution of liquor, tobacco products and other consumer goods, for sale to the British who were serving in Madras. In fact, the agency set up a warehouse near Fort St George, the seat of administrative power of the Madras Presidency. In 1898 the business was incorporated as a company, with an initial capital of Rs 8 lakh and with 4,000 preferred shares and 4,000 common shares. The principal shareholders were A.M. Hooper, G.D. Coleman and G.A. Ruppell.

Vittal acquired the company in the early days of Independence. Very soon, restrictions began to be clamped on imports of various kinds, including liquor, as a measure to promote domestic industry. While there was demand for foreign liquor, the supplies were restricted. To cater to this demand, Vittal and other liquor businessmen began to promote the stuff they distilled or brewed as Indian Made Foreign Liquor (IMFL). They thought this would be appealing to the consumer, who would at least be satisfied that he was drinking a close substitute for the real thing. The term IMFL caught on and is still in vogue.

McDowell established its first distillery in 1959 in Cherthala on the banks of the Vembanad lake that spans many districts in Kerala. The concentrates were first imported for the distillery. The first products were Bisquit brandy and Dorville French brandy, followed by extra neutral alcohol (ENA). The company launched its first original product, McDowell's No. 1 brandy, in 1963-64. McDowell's No. 1 whisky was introduced only in 1968. In between, in 1965, the company had acquired Carew & Company and Phipson & Company that manufactured rum, gin and other hard liquors. Carew & Company, based out of Calcutta, were producers of one of the finest rums in British India. Their products were endorsed by officials as high placed as the Viceroy of India.

Vittal's dream was to establish an end-to-end liquor empire that was also the largest in the country. To that end he commissioned new distilleries in Hyderabad in 1969, in Ponda (Goa) in 1971 and in Hatidah (Bihar) in 1975. In the early 1970s, Mallya also acquired Herbertsons Ltd, a liquor distribution company.

The aftermath of the Emergency brought the Janata government to power, and with Gandhian Morarji Desai as prime minister, the first steps towards prohibition were taken. Liquor manufacturers went into a tizzy. In panic they began to exit the business, fearing they would be ruined totally if they continued. But Vittal Mallya was made of sterner stuff; he reasoned that prohibition would not continue for long and began buying breweries and distilleries that were now being sold cheap! He took up management contracts for many breweries like Premier, Jupiter, Punjab and Indo-Lowenbrau, and for distilleries in Udaipur, Alwar, Mirganj and Serampore. He also set up a plant in Pondicherry. With all these acquisitions Mallya became the largest manufacturer and distributor of beer and IMFL in India, beating the incumbent market leader Mohan Meakin. However, the north-based Mohan Meakin's Golden Eagle beer still outsold the beers from the UB stable.

Vittal, now at the top of his industry, would still not take it easy. He continued the process of consolidation. He sought and got two acres of land on lease from the Jammu and Kashmir government to start a hops' nursery. He gave seedlings to the farmers and bought up their entire crop. With this move of backward integration, he acquired control of the most vital ingredient for beer manufacture.

Vittal's ambitions, however, extended beyond liquor and beer. In those days, the liquor business was not considered very respectable. One does not know whether his decision to diversify into other businesses had anything to do with this. But it is also a fact that the market was small, consumption of liquor being limited to the upper middle classes. The poor got their kick from locally brewed stuff like arrack. This may have also influenced his decision to diversify.

In 1950, he acquired a food company, Kissan Products, giving him access to a huge range of ketchups and jams. The company had been founded in 1935 by the Mitchell brothers, primarily to cater to the culinary demands of the British settler. But with the British leaving India the company was also up for sale, and Vittal bought it. In fact, this was his general strategy then: to acquire companies being sold by the British who wanted to go back home.

When Vittal took over Herbertsons in 1973 and made it a fully owned subsidiary of UB, the Dipy's division, which was in the food business, came along with it. This gave him a virtual stranglehold in the processed foods market—of jams, lime juice concentrate and other similar products. Dipy's (originally D&P Products P. Ltd) was in 1969 amalgamated with Herbertsons. Founded in 1913, Dipy's had started off as an importer and distributor of liquor and processed foods. It had a factory near Bhandup in Bombay (now Mumbai).

Herbertsons had launched its own brand of brandy, Honey Bee, in 1974, and followed it up with Bagpiper whisky in 1976, which in a few years' time became the largest selling whisky in the country.

With his passion for analysing balance sheets and identifying companies ripe for takeover, Vittal was able to buy into a huge range of companies owned by British businessmen poised to exit India. Two of them were Malayalam Plantations and Bush Boeke Allen, whose boards he entered. In fact, he became the chairman of Malayalam Plantations, as also of companies such as British Paints, Indian Sewing Machines and Cadbury India. He became the chairman of British Paints through Hoechst AG, which had taken over Berger Paints, which in turn happened to be the parent company of British Paints in India. In similar fashion, using Cadbury-Schweppes, the international associates of Kissan Products, he became the chairman of Cadbury India too.

In 1956, he co-promoted Hoechst Pharmaceuticals in association with Hoechst AG of Germany, a company that currently exists as Sanofi India. He also bought over Hindustan Polymers (from the Shrirams) and Mysore Electro Chemical Works, manufacturers of batteries.

By 1981, Vittal controlled ten breweries, fourteen distilleries, seven processed food companies, six investment companies, two small packaging units, three drug firms, a battery unit and some soft drink bottling plants. His business empire was worth Rs 350 crore—a conglomerate of a substantial size for those days. However, besides being extremely low-key, he ran his companies in near total secrecy. Nobody outside knew anything much about his empire.

He was not only self-effacing but also extremely cost conscious. His offices were not grand—in fact, they were not even carpeted and were rather barely furnished. He had a flat structure for his organization, where hierarchy was non-existent. He knew all his staffers, and with his obsession for cutting costs he insisted that all the company vouchers for expenses be sent to him. When he travelled to other cities, he was not ready to stay in luxury hotels, choosing more modest accommodation. He was a modest drinker himself and a workaholic to boot. Stories of his penny-pinching ways are legend at UB House.

'He was miserly and went to great lengths to save money. Those were days of telegrams, which would be charged by the number of words. To save money he would sign off as Vittalmallya in one word. Moreover, he would never say "Regards" at the end to save costs,' an old-timer remembers. He adds: 'When he was out touring he would ask his secretaries to set up appointments in such a way that he did not have to travel zigzag or tack up and down the same route. All this was to save costs.'

Needless to add, with such a cost regime in place, his staffers were not at all well paid. 'Some old-timers like Srinivasa Rao, who was one of the chief lieutenants of Vittal Mallya, were there when I joined in 1987. They were very conservative and old-school and were focussed—obsessed, rather—with controlling costs,' says V. Subramanian, who was Vijay Mallya's executive secretary.

In its story on Vittal Mallya, published a year before his death in 1983, *India Today* wrote: 'The strategy of growth through acquisitions underlines Mallya's basic business asset: financial wizardry. He can see through any balance sheet in five minutes, say his bankers, and others testify that he can merely look at the figures and decide whether the company is ripe for a takeover.'

The story also said: 'But Mallya is also very much the sick unit specialist, the industrialist with Midas touch producing the most memorable managerial success after taking over floundering companies. Every brewery he has picked up in recent years has been turned around by pumping in money to modernise machinery and then getting it to manufacture his popular brands, Kingfisher and UB lager.'

Possibly on account of his punishing work schedule, Vittal's health began to fail pretty early on in life. His eyes were bad, and poring over reports in small print probably affected his vision even more, requiring him to use more and more powerful spectacles. Then, he had a heart attack, presumably brought on by the constant touring and the stress of looking after his myriad businesses. Vittal was only thirty-nine at the time. Thus it was that in 1965 he shifted back to Calcutta. He had shifted with his family to Bangalore in 1958 to look after the business that was centred on the Garden City. The move back to Calcutta was to allow him to slow down. But it is doubtful if he ever did slow down.

He also had a passion for cars and owned many high-end vehicles. But with his obsession for keeping expenses on a leash, many of them remained parked and were seldom taken out.

Vittal had married Lalita Ramaiah in the early 1950s and had by her his only son, Vijay. But we have it on the testimony of Vijay that his father moved out of their home to live with a woman who already had grown-up children. The identity of this lady is not known. In an interview to the *Times of India*'s Bangalore edition, published on 20 April 2002, Vijay Mallya said: 'My father married thrice. The first lady my father started living in with had two grown-up daughters. There were times when they would drive down to buy *paan* in a Merc and I was around. I didn't care so long as I got my *paan*.'

Much later, Vittal met Kailash Advani, a garment manufacturer in Bombay who was a lawyer by education. Kailash was much younger than Vittal, but the two decided to get married. After the marriage, she changed her name to Ritu Mallya, apparently on astrological advice. She had also been previously married and had children from the earlier marriage.

Vittal may have been a much married man but he was clear that he had only one heir and that was his only son, Vijay. Although Vittal lived in Bangalore (he returned to live there) and Vijay in Calcutta, the father tried to keep the son under his control. In the same interview to the Bangalore edition of the *Times of India*, Vijay reminisced about his father as a tough taskmaster. Apparently, Vijay was a middling student who stood fifteenth in a class of thirty at school. One day, when Vijay was in class nine, Vittal told him that his low rank in class was not acceptable to him: 'I used to come first in class, so your performance has also to improve. Otherwise there is no way that United Breweries will come to you.' Vijay was jolted by this, and soon his academic performance showed great improvement.

Being socially conservative, Vittal was not gender-sensitive, like many of his generation. In the late 1970s, the daughter of UB's head brewer Rasendra Mazumdar approached him for a job as a brewer. Mazumdar and Vittal were neighbours, so the young woman was known to the latter. Moreover, she had studied malting and brewing in the University of Ballarat in Australia and had also worked in Australia and in India as a brewer. But Vittal said: 'You know you are a very bright lady. But this is not a woman's job. We can't take you into UB because men will feel uncomfortable working with you.' No amount of pleading helped. The young lady is known today as the Biocon founder, Kiran Mazumdar-Shaw.

Vittal Mallya died at the relatively young age of fifty-nine after a massive heart attack on 13 October 1983. 'Just back from escorting a group of British collaborators to Nepal's Tiger Tops and en route to Goa for a brief business vacation with other collaborators, Mallya was attending a Cathay Pacific Airlines cocktail party at Bombay's Taj Mahal hotel when he suffered a massive cardiac arrest resulting in instantaneous death,' read his obituary in *India Today*.

The obituary also carried an apt description of Vittal: 'He died as he lived, on the go. A restless nomad whose normal monthly schedule involved at least ten inter-city and sometimes inter-continental hops, Vittal Mallya at 59 maintained the same tireless pace which had helped him to build a massive industrial empire in 35 years.'

4

The Initial Years

VIJAY MALLYA WAS IN New York on official work when he received the news that his father had suddenly passed away. He rushed back to Bangalore, where Vittal Mallya's embalmed body had been brought from Mumbai. It was Vijay's stepmother Ritu who received him on his arrival.

Vittal had not formally anointed Vijay as his successor, but it was clear to everyone that this was what he wanted. Vijay had been appointed as a director at United Breweries in early 1974, upon his turning eighteen, the permissible age for directorship according to Indian Company Law. By this time, Vijay was at St Xavier's College in Calcutta, studying for a B.Com degree. Classes here were from 6 a.m. to 10 a.m., and this meant the young man had a lot of free time during those days. Vijay had been encouraged to work at the offices of UB in Calcutta for some on-the-job training, for which he received a small stipend too.

Later, after his graduation, Vijay was packed off to places like Shahjahanpur to learn the ropes at the lowest level. Life was difficult for him in such remote places. 'All I had for transportation was a cycle and the nearest cinema hall was 12 miles away,' Vijay reminisced in an interview many years later. But this grind gave him an experience of real life. Later on he was deputed to New York to get a taste of international business life; here he worked at Hoechst, whose Indian subsidiary had been co-promoted by Vittal Mallya. Vijay went on to work at the headquarters of UB in Bangalore too.

Vijay had been learning fast, but the consensus among the management was that at twenty-seven he was not yet ready to take up Vittal's mantle. In the flat structure through which he had operated, Vittal had two or three close confidants like M. Srinivasa Rao (who had turned around many of the sick breweries and distilleries that had been taken over) and H.P. Bhagat (under whose tutelage Vijay had taken his baby steps at the company). Many felt that one of the two should head UB after Vittal's sudden death. Others thought that even if Vijay was appointed as the head, he should have a regent who would guide him for a few years. Vijay had already built a reputation for being a party animal, for his extravagant ways and for his fondness for members of the fair sex. This, in the eyes of many who knew him well, was good enough reason why he should be on probation.

In this scenario, when a general meeting of shareholders of UB was held, they started loudly voicing their opinion that Vijay should be crowned as the chairman. Most of them did not know Vijay personally, but for them the fact that he was Vittal's son was good enough reason for his appointment. If the father was dead then his legal heir was the son. That's how it always was in India and there was no scope for anybody else to be appointed, went their opinion. A regent could be appointed if the son was a minor. But Vijay was grown up and needed no regent. Thus it was that Vijay was voted in as the new boss of United Breweries.

But it was hardly roses all the way for him. For starters, his father's colleagues who had expected to take over from Vittal were still around. It was not easy for him to extend his leadership over them or for them to accept his overlordship. Then, Vittal and Vijay were as different as chalk and cheese. Vittal was very cost conscious and monitored every single paisa that was spent; he was a very enterprising man but at the same time carefully planned his moves. This left no scope for him or his company to be compromised. Vijay had been taught the process of reining in expenses after working in UB, but he was not frugal. He thought big; grand ideas attracted him.

The brand of Kingfisher beer, now known across the globe, was launched by UB in 1978 during Vittal's time. Rummaging through the files and other papers in UB's Bangalore office, Vijay had found that the Kingfisher label had belonged to one of the predecessor companies since 1857. But the logo of the bird was in black and white and done very plainly. Vijay proposed to his father that the bird be redrawn to highlight its colourful plumage and that the company spend money branding Kingfisher to achieve a quantum leap in sales of the beer. Not surprisingly, Vittal rejected the idea.

But once he was at the helm, Vijay began to give shape to this idea. It also made a lot of sense for him to concentrate on Kingfisher because UB was still trailing Mohan Meakin in the beer segment. The latter's Golden Eagle outsold Kingfisher.

He wanted to use the vibrant colours of the kingfisher, a bird known for its keen instinct and perfect aim, to brand the beer. The vibrant colours and other characteristics of the bird would reflect energy, youthfulness, enthusiasm and freedom, leavened by a touch of formality and discipline. As a rookie during his father's time, Vijay had even organized a survey of college students to figure out their preferences, and that is where the idea of a youth connect for Kingfisher had occurred to him. Pitting a colourful Kingfisher against a Golden Eagle also helped. After all, the eagle was fierce and rough. In contrast, the kingfisher looked a friendly and attractive bird.

Kingfisher had begun to be exported to the UK in 1982, and to the US in 1983. Vittal was very much at the helm then. The exports were in the traditional 650 ml bottle. The brand rapidly gained a toehold in Indian restaurants in these two countries. In the UK it became such a success that production for that market had to be shifted there in three years' time. Shepherd Neame, Britain's oldest brewer of 1698 vintage, was chosen to produce Kingfisher under licence and specification at their brewery in Feversham in Kent. A little later, local production of Kingfisher was started in the US too. Mendocino Brewing Corporation, renowned as the brewer of full-bodied traditional beers and pioneer of the American craft brewing renaissance, was chosen. Unlike Shepherd Neame, this California-based company was new and had state-of-the-art facilities. By 1997, Vijay Mallya had acquired the company.

In 1985, he began to eye Shaw Wallace & Company, one of the largest liquor companies in India. The story goes that he got wind of Bangalore-based Khoday group's interest in buying out the foreign equity of Shaw Wallace. This made him sit up, as he realized that if this happened he would be left behind in the industry. The Shaw Wallace acquisition story demonstrates how differently Vijay and Vittal approached business. A typical Vittal operation was the acquisition of Punjab Breweries. This brewery was run by the legendary M.S. Oberoi of the Oberoi group. The company was not doing well, one of the reasons being continuous interference by the state government, which happened to be one of the shareholders. Oberoi was frustrated, and more so because running a brewery was not his primary business. So in 1978, when prohibition was brought in, he was ready to sell out. At this point, Vittal, who had been eyeing the company, approached him and picked it up for a song.

But Shaw Wallace, a *box-walla,* blue-chip, cash-rich company, was not up for sale—at least, its Indian management was not willing to let go of the company. But Vijay had a soft corner for the company, and not the least because it was based out of Calcutta. Having grown up in that city he knew how much awe the name of Shaw Wallace evoked; more than what United Breweries commanded in Bangalore at that time. To acquire Shaw Wallace was his dream.

With the help of a non-resident Indian, Manu Chhabria, the young inheritor mounted a bid on the company. He himself remained in the background. This was the kind of takeover bid that Vittal would never have made, although he himself was known as a takeover maestro. Vittal would only consider companies whose fundamentals were weak and were prime candidates for takeover.

Shaw Wallace was founded in 1886 by David Shaw and Charles Wallace. It owned top brands like Royal Challenge, Hayward's (named after the last British chairman of the company, Sir Anthony Hayward), Director's Special,

Antiquity, Old Tavern rum, and the brandies Golconda and John Exshaw.

Manu Chhabria, a Sindhi businessman, had started his career on Bombay's Lamington Street, a market that dealt in smuggled electronics goods (in those days, import curbs resulted in a flourishing market for smuggled goods). Having done well in Bombay, Manu, an ambitious man, shifted to Dubai and founded a company called Jumbo Electronics that became an importer of electronic products made by Japan's Sony. Soon, Jumbo had become the largest importer of Sony's goods in the UAE.

Vijay was introduced to Manu through a common acquaintance. Vijay proposed that they jointly bid for Shaw Wallace. At this point—in early 1985—Manu had no clue what Shaw Wallace was all about. But Vijay sold the idea well to Manu, who was in the news for having acquired another redoubtable multinational company based out of Calcutta a few months ago. In association with R.P. Goenka of the Goenka group, Manu had bid for Dunlop and taken it over at the end of 1984.

Vijay's interest in roping in Manu was the same reason for which R.P. Goenka had roped him in for Dunlop. In those pre-liberalization days, Indian companies could not buy companies or equity abroad. India was woefully short of foreign exchange, and the government was not ready to allow use of this precious resource for buying equity.

In the case of Shaw Wallace, Vijay had heard that one of its foreign owners was willing to part with their holding as they needed the cash for something else. Vijay would now require somebody else—who was an NRI and not subject to restrictive Indian laws—to front-end his acquisition. He zeroed in on Manu without properly checking his antecedents. If a traditional business baron like R.P. Goenka was comfortable dealing with Manu, he was safe too, thought Vijay. Had he done his homework properly he would have discovered that Manu was highly ambitious and ruthless to the core. He trusted very few people and was well known for his outbursts at his managers. Manu had cut his teeth on the streets, so to speak, and was poles apart culturally from Vijay. In fact, Manu fell out with R.P. Goenka too later.

The owners of R.G. Shaw & Company, which owned 38.7 per cent of Shaw Wallace, were ready to sell out. To acquire these shares, Manu Chhabria resorted to an indirect way: he used a company he owned in Singapore called Keysberg to buy up an existing shell company called Carrasco that was registered in Hong Kong. Carrasco then bought the shares offloaded by R.G. Shaw. The whole deal was for $26.14 million, and Carrasco obtained a $15 million loan from American Express to part-finance the transaction. The remaining $11.14 million was brought in directly by Chhabria. It was rumoured that Vijay had himself part-financed the money that Chhabria had brought in (through a complex web of transfers). It was also rumoured that Vijay and Manu had jointly bought Carrasco. Whatever the truth was, the moment it was known that Manu had bought the shares, all hell broke loose at the Calcutta headquarters of the company. The top management, led by its chairman and managing director, S.P. Acharya, was incensed. In effect the company was a managerial firm, and it was the top executives who ran it. The shareholders sitting abroad were happy with the dividends they got and did not interfere with its running.

A takeover was going to affect the managers most, breaking their hegemony in the company. Acharya—who had risen up the ranks from the position of assistant accountant—decided to oppose the takeover by all means. For starters, information was passed to the regulatory authorities, to the income tax department and to the ED about the suspected hand of Vijay Mallya in organizing the takeover. Then, Acharya and his managers refused to call for any general body meeting for eighteen long months and did not register the SWC shares bought by Manu. Thus, Manu came in possession of the shares but was not able to exercise his authority as owner of the shares.

The Indian authorities needed just one good tip to go after Vijay Mallya. He was arrested one evening—in June 1985—as he landed in Bangalore from Calcutta. He had to spend one night in the custody of the ED before he was let off on bail the following morning. But his passport was impounded. None of this chastened him, though. Addressing a press conference after his release, he said: 'Arrest should be the last resort. I never absconded.' He also told newspersons who met him separately: 'People are jealous of the successful. I am successful.' ED officials, meanwhile, insisted they had not picked up a millionaire at the airport for nothing. They said Mallya's passport had been impounded for fear that he might travel abroad and attempt to destroy evidence and influence potential witnesses.

After months of investigations, the ED in July 1986 filed a criminal complaint charging Chhabria, his brother Kishore and Vijay Mallya with having conspired to acquire 38.7 per cent of Shaw Wallace in violation of the provisions of the Foreign Exchange Regulation Act. The charge sheet specifically said: 'Shri Vijay Mallya with Shri M.R. Chhabria acquired a company called Carrasco Investment Limited.'

For a long time the government did not instruct its directors on the board of Shaw Wallace as to whose side they should take, whether they should support the existing management or the raiders. (Actually, these directors were not direct government appointees but nominees of public financial institutions controlled by the government, so effectively they were like government directors.) As a result, the nominee directors of the financial institutions who owned a chunk of shares in Shaw Wallace (as they did in most of the public companies in those times) remained inert. In effect, they ended up supporting the status quo, or the existing management led by Acharya.

All this while Manu Chhabria did not sit quiet either. He moved the Calcutta High Court, alleging that Acharya and some of his other colleagues were stripping Shaw Wallace of its assets and that some of the brands of the company were being transferred to private parties. He also approached the Company Law Board, complaining that Shaw Wallace was refusing to register his shares in the company.

Ultimately, in May 1987, Chhabria was able to wrest control of Shaw Wallace and enter the board of the company. By this time the investigations of the law enforcement agencies had also ended. Nothing amiss could be proved. But this was not the end of the story. Vijay now demanded that he should be made the co-owner of the company because this had been a joint operation. But the wily Manu flatly refused. He pointed out that Vijay had no papers to prove that he had anything to do with the deal. In fact, Vijay had denied before the ED—when its investigations were on—that he had anything to do with Shaw Wallace or Chhabria. He had also claimed that he did not co-own Carrasco even while Manu had declared before the ED officials that he was the sole owner of Carrasco. So how could Vijay now claim that he was a partner in the takeover? He could do nothing but eat humble pie, that too in silence. He had committed a blunder, he realized. He now resolved two things: first, it was very important to be an NRI, and second, he would take over Shaw Wallace one day, come what may.

Many a critical whisper from those who had been sceptical about his elevation as the chairman and managing director at UB could now be heard saying: 'We told you so.' 'He is not fit to be the boss.' 'He does not even have common sense.' 'He is taken in by what his *chamchas* say.' The last bit was a reference to the large entourage that perpetually surrounded the industrialist. Most of them were his friends from school or college. The perception of the sceptics also strengthened with the fiasco that two other new businesses started by Mallya ended in.

Foreseeing that a pizza and fast food revolution in India was around the corner, Vijay decided to set up a food chain soon after taking over the UB group. Styled McDowell's Pizza King, the fast food chain served three sizes of pizza with two types of bases—thin and thick. The outlets also served grilled sandwiches and had a salad bar. The first of them opened in New Delhi's Connaught Place to huge queues. Buoyed by this, he soon ordered more outlets to be opened—not only in Delhi but also in Mumbai. In his estimation, the market in Mumbai was twice that in Delhi. This was no estimate but his gut feeling arising from overconfidence at the Delhi outlet's successful opening. Between Delhi and Mumbai, fifteen outlets of McDowell's Pizza King were in operation, but most of the outlets in Mumbai had little business on weekdays. On weekends, however, they did roaring business. In the 1980s, eating out had not caught on as it has today. On weekdays most people preferred to eat at home. At lunch time too, the fact that Mumbai had a great *dabba* delivery system meant that office-goers did not need to venture out to restaurants. In other words, the *dabbawalas* foiled the pizza business. The outlets in Mumbai were mostly operating on a franchisee model, and the franchise owners started giving them up because their fixed costs for renting the premises was high, and business was not big enough to cover the rents.

There were other problems too. Vijay's trouble with the government agencies over the Shaw Wallace matter took the focus away from this business. There wasn't enough money to pump into the venture either. In the end, he wound it up in 1987.

The other fiasco regarded a 'cola type' of drink that he wanted to sell. After Coca-Cola was told to pack up from India in 1977 by the Janata government, there was no equivalent drink in the Indian market. Soft drinks like Campa Cola had been introduced, but they were poor substitutes for Coca-Cola. The ambitious Vijay Mallya thought he would try his hand in this market that missed a good product. He came out with a drink called Thril (spelt with a single l.) He hired a leading actress of the time, Rati Agnihotri, to model for its advertisements. One of the ads can be seen on the Internet, on a site showing popular ads of the 1980s; it features a young and pretty Rati sipping the cola, the slogan saying 'Share My Thril'. The lines below say: 'The great Cola taste of Thril – Has got the stars sparkling.' The ad was good but failed to attract. Consumers found Thril a dud drink, and it bombed in the market.

In the early 1990s, he also tried to bring MTV to India. 'He had set up an internal team to facilitate the entry. But due to foreign exchange regulations, we could not get RBI clearance and thus the effort did not fructify,' says a Mallya manager who was part of the team.

Thus the things Vijay Mallya dabbled in during his early years in business were quite varied and he was seldom successful until he came into his own through much trial and error.

5

A Finger in Every Pie

VIJAY MALLYA WAS A young man in a hurry. One would have expected the Shaw Wallace experience to have left him chastened. But nothing of the kind happened. Undeterred by that setback, he was now searching for new avenues for acquisition. He wanted to prove to the world that he was not the worthless heir that many around him had thought him to be. He soon found a new interest—engineering. He fathomed that a liquor magnate had less respect in society than a businessman running an engineering conglomerate. He decided that the way forward was through engineering and petrochemicals. The latter, in fact, was a greenfield area. He was probably inspired by the engineering giant Larsen & Toubro, which had the reputation of being a rock-solid, diversified engineering group, or by Dhirubhai Ambani, whose rapier-sharp forays into the petrochemical industry were creating waves.

Mallya's attention was drawn towards Best & Crompton, a Madras-based engineering company that had a British ancestry but now was in need of care. Founded in 1879 as a partnership firm by Andrew Vans Dunlop Best, it later became a managing agency that looked after Crompton Engineering, also based in Madras. In April 1974, the two companies merged to become Best & Crompton. The company was managed by professionals, and most of the equity (56 per cent) was held by public financial institutions. It had no owner as such and many Indian groups were eyeing the company, a manufacturer of industrial and agricultural pumps, lifts, mini-generators and power transmission cables. In going for Best & Crompton, Mallya tried to ape the strategy of his father, who always targeted English-owned companies that were not doing well.

Among those interested in Best & Crompton were the L.M. Thapar group of Delhi and the M.V. Arunachalam-led TI group of Madras. But Mallya was one up on them; he slowly but steadily (again in line with his father's strategy) bought shares of B&C from the market, achieving a 17 per cent equity ownership in the company over six months. At this point he demanded a position on B&C's board, which he said was justified because of his substantial shareholding. The financial institutions—Unit Trust of India, General Insurance Corporation of India and Life Insurance Corporation—which collectively held the majority shares in B&C were game. Not only did they offer Mallya and one of his representatives a place on the board of B&C but also actually handed over the company's management to him. This was some time in 1989. The financial institutions' decision was probably guided by the fact that the professional management at B&C was faltering. The company could do well with an owner at the helm, they thought, especially because it was badly in need of cash. Once a major player in the Gulf market, the company had experienced a pile-up of dues due to a slump. This had badly affected its cash flow and consequently its ability to implement projects.

Earlier, in November 1988, Mallya had acquired a controlling interest in Western India Enterprises (WIE), a Pune-based construction and erection company that was started as a partnership firm by two foresighted technocrats. The company had gone public in 1972 and had a good name in the market. Mallya, while taking over the company, was reported to have said: 'We have identified engineering as a promising area for diversification. WIE will help us in-house in setting up petrochemical projects that we propose to establish. With our support WIE can grab a major share of the construction contracts.' Later, the company's name was changed to UB Engineering. The firm is still with the UB group. As an EPC (engineering, procurement and construction) contractor implementing projects on a turnkey basis, the company used to make a small profit year after year. However, it has slipped into heavy losses over the last few years, and its turnover has sharply fallen too.

In 2014-15, the last year for which its annual report is available, UB Engineering made a loss of Rs 161.58 crore on a turnover of Rs 118.36 crore. The company's net worth is negative—which means its losses have eroded its equity and whatever earlier profits it may have had in its reserves. The turnover for 2014-15 is not even a third of the turnover of Rs 304.8 crore recorded in 2013-14. Announcing its annual results, the company said its fortunes had dipped as it did not have enough cash and the banks were not ready to lend money to it. This means it was unable to implement the orders it had in hand. So precarious is the situation that UB

Engineering is now on its way to the Board for Industrial and Financial Reconstruction (BIFR). Sick companies are referred to the BIFR, which determines whether their revival should be expedited if it finds them viable, or their closure expedited if unviable. Perturbed by these developments, Mallya was looking for a buyer for UB Engineering when he left for London in March 2016.

Best & Crompton, however, was sold within a few years of his taking over that company. B&C was facing severe labour problems; its workers began to refer to Mallya as a non-performing asset (NPA) within a year or two of the takeover. They said he had done nothing to improve the performance of the company. The investors too were not happy with his leadership of B&C. He ultimately sold it to an Indonesian company. Even before this, B&C's stake in an elevator manufacturing joint venture called Beacon Kone was sold off to the joint venture partner, the Kone group of Finland.

However, Mallya's own managers think he had a great understanding of what was happening at B&C. Rajan Ranganthan, the CFO at B&C, who was earlier Mallya's executive assistant, recollects how banks and financial institutions were mighty impressed with his performance at the company. He remembers how, for a meeting with bank/financial institution managers on B&C, Mallya arrived straight from the airport, speedily flitting through a sixty-slide presentation. He spoke for an hour—and so eloquently that the bankers immediately granted him whatever he wanted.

Mangalore Chemicals & Fertilizers (MCF), located just north of Mangalore, was another company that caught Mallya's fancy. This was a company which had been given a licence to manufacture chemical fertilizers (basically urea and other ammonia-based fertilizers) in 1966. The original promoter, the little-known Duggal Enterprise from Delhi, had tied up with the International Development and Investment Company Limited of Nassau in the Bahamas, the third partner being the government of Karnataka. But the promoters withdrew from the project in 1969, leaving it to the state government to take the project forward. The government took up the task, first renaming the company, then known as Malabar Chemicals and Fertilizers, and then completing the project for which it was founded. In 1976, the company began production, marketing its urea under the brand name Mangala.

Since this company too was plagued by labour problems, power shortages and non-availability of raw materials, the state government decided to hand it over to a private promoter, which it felt would be in a better position to run the company. On the basis of bids called from private parties, the company was handed over to Mallya's UB group in 1990.

But Mallya had clearly bitten more than he could chew. Problems at MCF continued, what with more labour troubles and other setbacks. Soon the company was in the red.

In 1995, realizing that he had no expertise to run a fertilizer company, he roped in SPIC (Southern Petrochemical Industries Corporation) of Madras as co-promoter of the company. Jointly they would rehabilitate the company, it was suggested. But having made huge losses, the company was before the BIFR, which shot down the proposal to bring in SPIC. In 1996, the BIFR appointed IDBI as what they call in official parlance the 'operating agency' for a Rs 300 crore revival package for the company. At the same time, the BIFR also ruled that the management of the company had to be changed.

Eventually, however, management change was not insisted upon because the very next year the company showed an improvement in performance. Perhaps the Damocles' sword hanging over it had made all the difference. Three years later, the BIFR in a fresh order asked the UB group to make a comprehensive revival proposal showing the required finances fully tied up.

For a decade or so, nothing extraordinary happened at MCF, but each year the company posted a profit before tax. At the turn of the decade, around 2010, an upcoming fertilizer company, Deepak Fertilizers and Petrochemicals, promoted by Pune-based Shailesh Mehta, began to show interest in buying into the company. As Deepak Fertilizers began to pick up shares in MCF through its subsidiary SCM Soilfert Ltd, Mallya sat up. Realizing that after the collapse of Kingfisher Airlines he did not have the financial wherewithal to maintain control over MCF, Mallya tied up with well-known industrialist Saroj Poddar to ward off a takeover bid. Poddar, son-in-law of K.K. Birla, is head of Goa-headquartered Zuari Agro Chemicals, a company he inherited from his father-in-law. On Mallya's prodding, Zuari bought into MCF in late 2014. But before Zuari could consolidate its holdings, Mallya was almost ousted as the chairman of MCF. Not finding it possible to hold on to the position, he resigned, but was able to push his stepmother Ritu Mallya on the board of the company. His resignation resulted in the company's share price going up in the market! This was perhaps because banks saw him as a liability (by this time Kingfisher Airlines had collapsed) and were no longer ready to give loans to MCF so long as he was the head.

As Zuari started buying into MCF, it was first brought in as co-promoter of the company along with UB. Later, Zuari's stake in MCF increased, and now stands at over 53 per cent. Mallya's stake in the company is around 20 per cent. Clearly, any day Saroj Poddar can decide to officially kick the Mallyas out of MCF. In a clear sign that Zuari wanted to take control of the company, the managing director was changed at its insistence. Deepak Anand, who as Mallya's nominee was the managing director for ten years, was made a non-executive director, and Suresh Krishnan, a nominee of the Zuari group, inducted as the new managing director in 2015. Although Saroj Poddar is not a member of the board of MCF, his son Akshay is a director. S.R. Gupte, formerly vice-chairman of Kingfisher Airlines, was also ousted from the board of MCF.

Another unrelated business that Mallya was engaged in was paints. But this came to him as an inheritance. Berger Paints in India had been founded in 1923 as Hadfield's India, with its sole factory in Howrah in Bengal. At the end of 1947, it was acquired by British Paints (Holdings) of the UK and renamed British Paints (India). In 1976, FERA regulations forced foreign companies to dilute their shareholding in their Indian outfits. Finding itself in a bind, the company brought its shareholding down to 40 per cent, offloading shares to Vittal Mallya. The choice fell on him because the parent company had changed hands and now belonged to Hoechst, a company with which he had close ties and with which he had jointly set up Hoechst India. Vittal was then appointed as the chairman of British Paints (India). The company's name was changed to Berger Paints (India) in 1983. After some more dilutions, the company fell into the lap of the UB Group.

But Vijay Mallya understood little about the paints industry and was not focused on that business. The paints company was not doing too well. Although the company fetched good valuations and could attract a good price, its prospects were not very rosy. Realizing what lay ahead, Mallya announced its sale.

Not many were interested in buying him out, so in the end the liquor king settled for an unknown Marwari group. But then lady luck smiled on him. Two little-known Sikh brothers who ran a small paint company approached him, offering to buy Berger Paints. He told them they would have to better the deal agreed upon with the Marwari group. The Sikh brothers were keen on the company and offered a very high price. This was not surprising because they had been in the paints industry for a long time. Berger Paints was finally taken over by the Sikh brothers, the Dhingras, in 1991. They never made public how much they paid for Mallya's stake in it, but he, many years later, revealed that he had made a killing. He claimed to have made US$66 million in the deal. Using a currency exchange rate of Rs 30 to a dollar in 1991, this translates to Rs 396 crore.

———

Another company that Mallya sold was Hindustan Polymers, a firm acquired by his father. The Visakhapatnam company was established in 1951 to manufacture styrene monomer, polystyrene and its co-polymers. In 1978, it was taken over by Vittal Mallya and merged with McDowell & Company. In July 1997, Vijay sold it to Korea's LG group, which subsequently renamed it LG Chemicals (Private) Limited.

Vijay Mallya also exited from Aventis, where he held a stake of over 27 per cent. The Mallya ownership of shares of this company was courtesy Hoechst India that had been founded by Hoechst AG of Germany in association with Vittal Mallya, as mentioned earlier. UB used to own 40 per cent of Hoechst India shares and this led—through a complicated process of changes in the ownership of Hoechst AG—to its shareholding in Aventis. In March 2010, Mallya sold his entire shareholding for Rs 414 crore, according to newspaper reports. But he continued as the chairman of Aventis, which was later renamed Sanofi India. In April 2016, he stepped down from this position. He had been the chairman of Sanofi and its predecessor companies since December 1983, taking the position held by his father, and a board director there since December 1973, shortly after he turned eighteen.

Living in Bangalore, it was only predictable that Mallya would get sucked into the software industry, which came to define the city. On 28 February 2000, at the height of the dotcom boom, Mallya set up two companies signalling his entry into the business. Kingfisher.Net and Bluepearl Internet Group Limited were both floated to supply customized software, applications software, computer software games, software publishing and consultancy. Neither company went anywhere.

In July 1994, as Bangalore was showing signs of rapid expansion, Mallya floated UB Transit Systems, his ambition being to run an elevated light rail transit system to provide faster transportation in the Garden City. Old Bangaloreans remember the buzz about the project at the time; it was billed as the first example of private–public partnership. For this reason there was a lot of opposition to it too. Mallya tied up with many international companies, giving them equity; he was in talks with Siemens, the Ansaldo group, ABB and GEC Alsthom. The private partners led by Mallya would own 75 per cent of the company's equity, and the Karnataka state government, through the Bangalore Metro Rail Transport Limited, 25 per cent. Though the project cost was pegged at Rs 4,200 crore and the project was supported by the J.H. Patel government then in power, Mallya could not provide a model showing that passenger fares would be reasonable. In the end, the project proposal came to naught because he wanted more funds from the state government, which was strapped for money as it was working on the Bangalore International Airport project that had been grounded for many years.

In 1995, Mallya also set up two companies to undertake mining. UB Mining and Mines (Exploration) India Limited were to mine non-ferrous metal ores other than thorium and uranium. Just a year earlier, he had established UB Resorts Limited to run hotels, camping sites and short-stay accommodations. Needless to add, all these companies remained on paper only. Most of them were established by him because he wanted to make use of the new opportunities now afforded by the economic liberalization that had opened up areas so far closed to the private sector.

In 1996, he started publishing an English newspaper, the *Asian Age,* from Bangalore. It was founded in Calcutta in 1996 and Mallya took up the franchise for publishing it from

Bangalore. The paper was the initiative of leading journalist M.J. Akbar. Mallya later bought up the franchise for the Kolkata edition too. However, a decade or so later he divested from both the editions and sold the rights to somebody else.

Many of the companies that Mallya started in the 1990s were folded up or taken over by UB (Holdings). But even companies taken over by UB (Holdings) and converted into divisions of the holding company continued to languish.

In 1985, soon after he inherited his father's empire, Mallya had launched Unitel Communications to manufacture and sell EPABX and telephones in partnership with Ericsson. This was soon after Rajiv Gandhi took over the reins of power at the Centre, taking halting steps towards liberalization, freeing telecom equipment manufacture for the private sector. Mallya came a cropper in this business also.

———

In the ultimate analysis, it is clear that Mallya's investments in engineering and allied activities flopped. But he was able to profitably sell most of the businesses that were started by his father and make money out of them. What his motivations were to exit some of these companies will be examined in the subsequent chapters. Analysts say that Mallya did not have the vision to venture beyond liquor and beer—one of the reasons why his airline crashed too.

'It requires a different sort of mindset to be successful in business, operating in many areas. Mallya did not have that; he was only geared towards liquor and beer,' says C. Shankar, a chartered accountant and corporate treasurer at a leading Bangalore-based corporation who has followed Mallya's businesses closely. Technocrat Prashant Sardessai agrees: 'Never have I encountered Mallya managers who were in the class of top-grade multinational managers. How could they run huge enterprises for him?'

Mallya was simply unable to assemble a diverse management team—a characteristic of big successful groups like the Tatas or Larsen & Toubro—that could oversee a diversified industrial empire.

6

Liberalization and After: Mallya's Spirited Rise

UNLIKE MALLYA'S OTHER VENTURES, his beer and liquor businesses did exceedingly well under him all through the 1990s. This was not surprising, overpowered as he was by his ambition to become the top Indian company in the business. With liberalization opening up the Indian economy, he gambled big time and went all out to compete with the global liquor giants.

'At that time the shares of his liquor companies used to quote in the double digits on the stock markets but his ambition was that they become so dominant that the stocks would quote at least Rs 1,000,' remembers Ram Mankekar, who was part of Vijay's corporate communication team. 'We were frequently subjected to his motivational talks about taking on the global leaders. He was himself very charged and did not consider the Indian liquor companies except Shaw Wallace to be competition. With such a high-energy boss who was on the job all the time, the team also strived to deliver results.' In the end, Mallya's efforts paid off, and by 2004 his company had become the fourth largest liquor company in the world after Diageo, Allied Domecq and Pernod-Ricard.

'I was confident that UB's beverage alcohol business had all the ingredients to be a world-class enterprise and globally competitive,' Mallya said in 2004 in an interview to *Pegasus*, his group's in-house magazine. 'The challenge was to stimulate world class thinking amongst my management and translate this into value enhancement of our products, distribution muscle and greater consumer confidence. When India's economic policies were liberalized in the early 1990s we made a decision to be globally competitive and world class. By the end of the '90s we were positioned in the international league and started setting our sights even higher. We persisted with product development and improvement concentrating on brand equity enhancement and growth.'

Although Indian industry as a whole had been clamouring for liberalization, once the doors were opened they went into a shell for some time. The fear of being swamped by foreign competition was uppermost in their minds and they conjured up visions of Indian groups getting wiped out, leaving an industrial landscape dominated by foreign brands. Some of the older businessmen also formed what was referred to as the 'Bombay Club', which called for protection of Indian companies. But liberalization was irreversible, although its pace was slow for some time. Realizing this, some Indian businessmen got their act together and braced themselves for the competition. They came out winners. Mallya was one of them.

Within a few years of taking over the empire in 1983, he began to consolidate his spirits business. This he achieved by taking up integrated marketing for the products of

McDowell and Herbertsons. Even joint brand campaigns for the companies' products were initiated. All this helped Mallya become a leading player in the Indian spirits market. That his rival companies like Mohan Meakin, Khoday's and Jagatjit Industries were ridden by internal tussles also helped. There were often too many family members involved in the business and this led to conflicts. But Mallya had no rivals internally: he had no brothers, and the entire business had been bequeathed to him by his father. He was the monarch of all that he surveyed, and to efficiently run his organization he had appointed professional managers. In the rival companies, managers, even if appointed, met with too much family interference. In Mallya's empire, the managers functioned under the overall supervision of the boss, but functionally they were free to operate.

By the end of the 1990s, Mallya had brought his entire liquor operations under one division and consolidated his leadership position in the business. In 1995, he merged Carew & Phipson and Consolidated Distilleries with McDowell. This left him with two companies for spirits: McDowell and Herbertsons. The two were brought together under unitary control, but the practice of maintaining two separate balance sheets for the two companies continued. This brought in what is called 'coopetition'—competition along with cooperation. These two companies could have been merged too, but there were many complications in the way even if Mallya wished to do this.

All these moves yielded results. By 1995, his company became the tenth largest producer of spirits in the world. And within just the next six years, it had entered the top-five league. According to *Impact International*, the New York-based news and research digest of the international beverage and alcohol industry, Mallya's company sold 26 million cases of liquor in 2001, behind only Diageo (93.2 million cases), Pernod Ricard (45 million cases), Allied Domecq (43.6 million cases) and Bacardi (34.2 million cases). Mallya's was not only the sole Indian company in the top league but also the only Asian company to make the grade. In 1995, there was a Japanese company, Suntory, on the list, but it soon fell by the wayside. In the Mallya inventory were seven millionaire brands—which meant that these seven spirit brands produced by his company sold more than 1 million cases each. When Mallya took up the reins at UB after the demise of his father in 1983, cumulative sales at the company were only 2.5 million cases annually.

What's interesting about Mallya's rise in the spirits business is that till the turn of the century he climbed the ladder by staying away from the winds sweeping the global spirits business. By and large, he did not stray out of the Indian market, barring forays into Nepal and West Asia. By contrast, most of the global majors were growing by buying companies in other countries. Mallya would resort to buying foreign companies only many years later.

Soon after liberalization was initiated, Mallya realized that foreign competition was at his doorstep. His McDowell & Company then tied up with a Scottish company, United Distillers Limited, to form United Distillers India Limited in 1992. The company began bottling one of the most well-known Scotch whisky brands in the world: Black Dog. This was the first joint venture in the alcoholic beverage industry in India. The whisky, with 42.8 per cent alcohol, was bottled in a facility in Nashik in Maharashtra.

Black Dog had a hoary ancestry. Launched for the first time in 1883 with the name Milard Black Dog by James McKinley of the Leith family of Scotland, it was brought to India by Walter Milard in 1906. The joint venture initiated by Mallya was to beat India's highly regressive tax structure. The company imported the spirit (the raw material) from Scotland and bottled it at a local Indian plant. This enabled it to circumvent the duty of 150 per cent levied on the import of the bottled drink. Under the arrangement, the government only levied a duty of 30 per cent on the domestically bottled drink.

A little over a decade later, Mallya took over Gilbey's Green Label, which was then the third largest brand of whisky in India, after Mallya's Bagpiper and Shaw Wallace's Director's Special. Gilbey's Green Label was a foreign brand that belonged to the largest liquor manufacturer in the world, Diageo. It was being produced in India by Diageo's subsidiary, UDV India.

The takeover took place in an indirect way. In the first stage, Deepak Roy, who had earlier been managing director of UDV, bought the brand at a price of Rs 60 crore. At that time, Green Label had a market share of 8 per cent in the domestic whisky market. Diageo wanted to shed Green Label so they could focus better on marketing their international brands like Johnnie Walker and Smirnoff vodka. However, the story doing the rounds was that the company was unable to profitably market Green Label in India. In the second stage, in December 2002, the UB group acquired 85 per cent of Triumph Distillers & Vinters Ltd at Rs 60 crore. This was the Roy-controlled company which had taken over Gilbey's Green Label, and along with it Gilbey's White whisky and

Gilbey's White Gold whisky. In 2005, Roy also sold his remaining 15 per cent stake in the company to the UB group and became an employee of Mallya's. This was a homecoming of sorts for him, having served with the group till 1995 as chief of Herbertsons.

In 2004, Vijay used Triumph to pick up liquor brands owned by the Indian-owned Polychem group. He picked up Alcazar vodka, Men's Club whisky, rum, brandy and gin, and Louis XI brandy. The brands sold little, but Mallya fashioned Alcazar to take on the leading vodka brand Smirnoff at half the price.

Meanwhile, the domestic market was expanding rapidly. This had much to do with the changing mindset of the urban Indian. Brought up in an India where drinking was considered taboo, not many ventured to drink Indian manufactured foreign liquor (IMFL). In rural India and among the lower income categories in the cities, there was always toddy, arrack and the like. The only group of Indians drinking was the westernized upper class and the rich. The Indian government's policies did nothing to popularize drinking either. In fact, the Directive Principles of State Policy in the Constitution of India say: ' ...the state shall endeavour to bring about prohibition of the consumption of intoxicating drinks.' High taxes and levies on liquor accounted for 65 per cent of their market price. Needless to say, this curbed the growth of the liquor market, which at the turn of the century would not have exceeded 10 per cent of the population.

Liberalization forced the government to moderate the high taxes on liquor, this in turn leading to increased demand for it. With the changing times, the conservatism in Indian society was also beginning to break down. In the earlier days, only men would drink, and that too in clubs. But now the taboo on women drinking was easing up, as also the taboo on drinking at home.

Indians are by and large whisky drinkers, which is contrary to the international trend. In Europe, wine and beer are preferred. The increasing trend in consumption of whisky was reflected in the sales of Mallya's whiskies. Sales of his numero uno brand Bagpiper consisted of 2 million cases in 1991, rose to 3 million cases in 1993, to 4 million cases in 1994 and to 5 million cases in 1998. By 2003, Bagpiper was selling 6 million cases and, by 2006, 10 million. This was a whisky that was introduced in the market in 1976.

McDowell's No. 1, the oldest whisky in the Mallya stable, had a similar success story. Introduced in the market in 1968, it was selling 1 million cases in 1991; sales shot up to 3.8 million cases in 2001 and to 6.1 million cases in 2005.

While sales of UB's branded spirits rose as a result of the market expanding, Mallya did a lot to push sales too. For starters, he was the first man to treat liquor as an FMCG (fast moving consumer good). Since advertisements for liquor were not allowed by the government, Mallya took recourse to surrogate advertising in a big way. McDowell also sold McDowell's No. 1 soda and McDowell's No. 1 water. McDowell's No 1 had a slogan, '*Mera Number 1*', and the brand (of soda and water, of course, but implying the whisky) was advertised at Bollywood, cricket, sports and music events. There were music concerts by Elton John, Enrique Iglesias and many Indian stars to boost the McDowell's No. 1 brand.

As a measure of product differentiation and to appeal to calorie-conscious consumers, a new variant of its whisky called McDowell's No. 1 Diet Mate was introduced. This was a world first. The product was introduced not only as a low-calorie whisky but also projected as one that boosted the drinker's metabolism.

The other brands in the stable were promoted in similar fashion. As early as 1993, Hindi film star Dharmendra was appointed as the brand ambassador for Bagpiper. The slogan of the advertisement was *'Khoob jamega rang jab mil baithenge aap, main aur Bagpiper'*. Other film stars—Ashok Kumar, Jackie Shroff, Sunny Deol, Shah Rukh Khan and Ajay Devgn—were roped in to promote Bagpiper at different times.

The salient features of each brand were exaggerated to give the advertisements a ring of realistic appeal. Thus, Gilbey's Green Label was pitched to people for whom life was still a struggle: *'Kuch paana hai, kuch kar dikhana hai'* were the lines promoting this brand, exhorting the drinker to achieve more to get more recognition in life.

———

Mallya also tried—and succeeded—in consolidating his beer business during this period. He unveiled newer brews and also went on an acquisition spree, picking up many smaller breweries across the country. He figured the time was ripe for foreign beer companies to enter India, and he wanted to maximize UB group's brewing capacity before their entry. Since the beer market across the country was fragmented—because different states had different policies—it made sense for his company to be present in as many states as possible, especially where demand for beer was high.

Post-liberalization, he also consolidated his beer

companies. In 1993, he amalgamated Punjab Breweries (acquired in 1979), High Range Breweries (set up in 1972 in Kerala), Kalyani Breweries (set up in 1960 in West Bengal) and Kesarwal Breweries (set up in 1965 in Goa) into United Breweries.

One of the most notable of his acquisitions was that of Associated Breweries in 2000. This was a company best known for its beer, London Pilsner, which dominated the Mumbai market. So strongly was it entrenched in the city that Mallya got a shock when he demanded Kingfisher at the Taj Mahal hotel and was refused; the hotel only stocked London Pilsner.

The company was run by three ladies—Zinia Lawyer, her mother Mehroo Irani and her sister Bhaktiyar Chenoy. Founded by the father, Noshirwan Irani, who built his fortunes in the construction business in south Mumbai, its first brewery was set up in Goa but later moved to the neighbourhood of Mumbai. After Noshirwan's sudden death in 1985, the three ladies took charge. Besides London Pilsner, the company also had other brews. London Diet was the first low-calorie beer in the country; then there was London Draft, and Maharaja Premium lager beer, which was exported to New Zealand, Japan and Australia. The name London was appended with the name of the brew to draw association with London's pub culture.

Mallya had had an eye on the company for a long time, but he moved post haste when he heard that SABMiller was doing due diligence of London Pilsner to consider its acquisition. Moreover, Associated Breweries had entered into an agreement with San Miguel of the Philippines to produce and market their brew in India. Mallya acquired 65 per cent of London Pilsner by offering an attractive price. On their part, the three ladies were willing to sell because they realized that competition was intensifying and they would stand no chance in the newly emerging scenario.

In 2001, Inertia Industries was acquired by a company floated by United Breweries. Inertia was based out of Delhi; it was started by the Tandon brothers in 1989. It had a brewery in Dharuhera in Haryana, but the prohibition policy in the state in the late 1990s badly affected operations. However, towards the end of the decade the company set up another brewery in Maharashtra. The company produced the Sandpiper brand of beer (a brew that was like mango-apricot-flavoured mild beer, tasting like water but a good thirst-quencher).

A year later, Mallya took over GMR Breweries in north coastal Andhra Pradesh. This was a strategic investment because Andhra Pradesh was one of the largest markets for beer. While his outfits had production facilities in other parts of Andhra Pradesh near Hyderabad–Secunderabad, they had none in north coastal Andhra, which seemed to be a market that could do with more beer. This market was also crucial for Mallya, if only for the fact that rival Shaw Wallace ruled there. GMR Breweries was also in prolonged negotiations with South African breweries for over two years, the price sought by the seller having delayed an agreement. In the end, Mallya jumped into the fray, offering over Rs 57 crore for the relatively new brewery.

A few months before the acquisition of GMR Breweries, he took over Mangalore Breweries in a most interesting way. This outfit, which produced the brands Lion King and Kolberg, was in a bad way, having piled up huge debts and was offering itself for sale. It was in negotiations with Shaw Wallace and had even entered into a memorandum of understanding (MoU) with that company; Shaw Wallace not only agreed to buy Mangalore Breweries but also to take over some of its debts. But having signed an MoU, Shaw Wallace was taking its own sweet time to fork out the cash. This alarmed the promoters of Mangalore Breweries, who now started talking to United Breweries. Mallya, whose mission was to maintain his number one status in the beer and spirits market in India, agreed to talk only because Mangalore Breweries was negotiating with his main rival. However, realizing the possible legal hurdles arising from the MoU having been signed, UB went slow. But fate intervened, and for some reason SWC was not able to close the deal. So in the end Mallya picked up the brewery and began using it to produce Kingfisher beer for the west coast and north Karnataka markets.

In 1999, Mallya floated a company in partnership with Ravi Jain, who had launched many brands for Shaw Wallace group as its managing director. Millennium Alcobev Breweries Limited (MABL) was to be a sister company of United Breweries, with its products flanking those of UB to bolster their market. (Alcobev stood for alcoholic beverage and intended to project the impression that beer was a beverage much like colas). All the underperforming brands that had been acquired by Mallya were to be transferred to the new company. Jain owned 39 per cent of the company, while for starters Mallya held 61 per cent. Jain's brief was to reposition all these brands through this new company, even as United Breweries would concentrate on Kingfisher. In line with this, MABL gave a new look to Sandpiper and repackaged it.

MABL also launched Zingaro, a strong beer for that market segment that preferred such a drink.

In 2001, Inertia Industries was given to MABL, which soon got into the business of acquiring new breweries. In 2002, MABL acquired Empee Breweries for $28 million. Thus two breweries, one each in Tamil Nadu and Kerala, and the brand Marco Polo came into the Mallya fold. This deal was intended to get the captive Tamil Nadu market under the UB belt. Government regulations in the state did not allow the market to be serviced by producers outside the state.

Later, in 2002, MABL entered into a joint venture with a British company, Scottish & Newcastle (S&N). The joint venture resulted in the introduction of mild beers produced by S&N like Kronenbourg, John Smiths, Newcastle, Brown Ale and Baltika. The joint venture with S&N was planned to stave off competition from Cobra beer and beers from Belgian Interbrew and Russian Sun Breweries. Cobra Beer belonged to Karan Billimoria, who was originally from Hyderabad but who had migrated to the UK. The first shipment of Cobra Beer was manufactured at breweries in Mysore and shipped to the UK. Thus, from Mallya's point of view, there was a great need to nip Cobra in the bud before it emerged as a competitor.

Another point of anxiety was South African Breweries (SAB), which had started its journey from Johannesburg in 1895. After dominating the African market for a few decades, the company expanded to Europe, North America and South America. It then acquired Miller, the second largest brewer in the US, and changed its name to SABMiller. After this it began to look aggressively for opportunities in China (which was a huge market) and India. This naturally made Mallya sit up and was perhaps responsible for his tie-up with S&N.

Though they collaborated operationally, UB and MABL were separate entities and were kept as such. Together they were twice the size of the next domestic competitor; together they owned nine brands, eleven breweries and had a market share of over 50 per cent. MABL had done well in bolstering languishing brands but had spent a lot on advertising, which made it a high-debt company. The costs of acquisition only added to its advertisement budget. Its debt burden at the end of 2005 was estimated to be over $20 million. This caused some dispute between Jain and Mallya, and in the end Jain's shares were acquired, partly by Mallya and partly by S&N. S&N became a 37.5 per cent partner in MABL. S&N was a 1749-vintage company headquartered in Edinburgh and was largely focused on Scotland and north England. But it expanded aggressively and became a leading player in the UK after some acquisitions in the mid-1990s. After that it expanded out of the UK and into western Europe and other territories. It was then that Mallya figured out that collaborating with S&N would make sense.

Even as Mallya was acquiring new breweries to increase UB's capacity, he was clear about his approach. He knew that in the beer segment Kingfisher was his main brand and would remain so in the future. So he was making all-out efforts to strengthen Kingfisher; United Breweries spent a huge amount of money on it for brand building.

Another innovative measure he took was to depict the kingfisher of the logo in a flying instead of a sitting position. This was to convey that the brand stood for dynamism. The packaging and the colour schemes were also changed to make them more attractive to the consumer. Kingfisher was positioned as a youth brand, and it sponsored robust and youthful activities, be they the derby, marathon or football. What was conveyed to the Kingfisher drinker was that he was young, exciting and fun-loving because that's what the beer was promoted as.

The Kingfisher swimsuit calendar featuring attractive models (which also launched leading actress Deepika Padukone) became an icon in itself. Youth figures like footballer Baichung Bhutia and racing driver Karan Chandhok (for Kingfisher Premium) promoted specific beer brands. Cricketer Vinod Kambli from Mumbai endorsed London Pilsner (essentially a Mumbai drink) and Bengali film hero Prosenjit endorsed Kalyani Black label beer (which was produced in West Bengal).

The Kingfisher Premium brand was strengthened by associating it with India Fashion Week and Kingfisher Fashion Awards. In some localities, Kingfisher indirectly promoted its beer by promoting pubs that largely served only Kingfisher brands. Kingfisher beer was also promoted in the UK through Indian restaurants as an accompaniment to Indian food, and the effort was successful.

United Breweries tried through other means too to promote its brews by making beer a drink for all seasons. This was to combat reduced sales during the monsoon months. Many sub-brands for Kingfisher were introduced: Kingfisher Strong, Kingfisher Lager (which was the leader in the low-alcohol segment, with an alcohol content of less than 5 per cent). To make a fashion statement, Kingfisher Premium had an Internet launch in Bangalore.

So it was that by 2005, nearly fifteen years into liberalization, Mallya had strengthened his position in both the spirits and beer markets. He was now ready to go for the kill and step out abroad to acquire companies.

On 17 May 2007, Mallya's United Spirits (formed after consolidation of his companies McDowell, Herbertsons and Triumph Distillers & Vintners), acquired a 100 per cent stake in Whyte & Mackay (W&M), a leading distiller of Scotch whisky. The amount paid: £595 million (Rs 4,800 crore). The company was based in Glasgow, so this was a case of an Indian enterprise going all the way to Scotland to acquire an outfit that produced Scotch.

The company with an ancestry that went back to 1850 had leading brands in its armoury, including The Dalamore, Isle of Jura, Glayva, Filtercairn, Vladivar vodka and Whyte & Mackay Scotch. It owned several other Scotch brands like John Barr and McKinley's. Although the acquisition was backed by sound business logic, Mallya was also swayed by the fact that his father had loved Isle of Jura.

Explaining the logic of the acquisition, he told the press: 'We have a large and growing business in India and have made recent forays into Russia and China. Until today the missing link has been Scotch, and due to shortages and rapidly increasing prices of Scotch whisky, we need a reliable supply source to secure our Indian brands considering that we use Scotch in our Indian blends.' W&M had a large Scotch distillery with a capacity of 40 million litres a year; it had four malt distilleries in all and a bottling plant. Its capacity could be doubled with an investment of £10 million.

Although he finally paid £595 million for the company, his original offer had been £475 million. He resisted raising this offer but was so keen on the company that he upped his ante and took a loan from ICICI Bank and Citibank to fund the purchase.

Almost a year before this, on 12 July 2006, he had acquired a wine manufacturer in France. Bouvet Ladubay SAS was located in the Loire Valley, a noted wine-producing region in France.

After tasting success in brewing beer and distilling whisky, Mallya was very keen to make his mark in wine. That was only natural because good sparkling wine was part of the lifestyle of a person who wanted to 'live life king-size'. He wanted to acquire vineyards in Bangalore and Nashik, but for some reason that did not work out. He then went to France, to the area known for the best vineyards, and sought to buy the well-known champagne conglomerate Taittinger.

His attempt to acquire Taittinger raised hackles in the area—not surprising, as most of the wine makers in the territory are family-owned enterprises. The locals felt an Indian group would only destroy the enterprise that had grown over a period of a few hundred years. In the end Taittinger did not sell out but it offered its subsidiary Bouvet Ladubay SAS to Mallya, who lapped it up.

Mallya paid €14.75 million to buy Bouvet Ladubay entirely. The company came along with its subsidiary Chapin Landais SAS. The acquisition was made by Asian Opportunities & Investments Ltd, a wholly owned subsidiary of United Breweries based in Mauritius. Bouvet Ladubay sold 3 million bottles of wine every year, raking up an annual revenue of €12 million.

According to an official statement, the acquisition was intended to introduce high-quality wines to the emerging wine connoisseur in India. It was also meant to enable Mallya-owned companies to take advantage of the distribution network of the company in Europe and the US to push their own products.

Mallya wanted to sell the wine in a big way in the UK by pushing it through Indian restaurants and supermarkets. He wanted to establish the acceptability of these sparkling brands in the UK in the same way that his Kingfisher brand had become acceptable in that country.

To broadcast the news of his acquisition and to popularize its wines, he held a mega wine-tasting event on his superyacht *Indian Empress* off the coast of Mumbai, where a select crowd, including leading industrialist L.N. Mittal and other top luminaries, was invited. He hoped goodwill for his newly acquired brands would now spread by word of mouth.

7

The Conquest of Shaw Wallace

ON 21 MARCH 2005, twenty years after he first started eyeing Shaw Wallace, Vijay Mallya finally bought over the spirits division of the company from the family of his bitter rival Manu Chhabria. The deal happened nearly three years after Chhabria's death in April 2002 and after his legal heirs lost the appetite to continue the feud any longer. Although one of Chhabria's daughters, Komal, was still in a mood to resist Mallya's acquisition of the company, his widow, Vidya, and his two other daughters decided to call it quits.

An exuberant Mallya immediately called up his mother, who lived in London, and told her about the conquest. The circumspect mother, very happy to hear about her son's success, is supposed to have said: 'What is destined will happen. Shaw Wallace was destined to be yours.'

There was palpable excitement in the city of Kolkata too. Shaw Wallace had an iconic status in the city, and goings-on in the company always made front-page news. For the past few years, the Chhabrias had been conspicuous by their absence; they were like absentee landlords, running their empire from faraway Dubai. Chhabria's untimely demise had also brought in an element of uncertainty about the fate of the company. 'What will happen to this blue chip company?' was the question on the minds of the city folk.

That an 'old Calcuttan', Vijay Mallya, was taking over the company pleased them. Mallya, however, kept the excitement going—possibly without intending to—by not showing up in Kolkata after the acquisition. It was a full six months later, in September, that he arrived at the Shaw Wallace headquarters in the city for the company's annual general meeting. With ecstatic employees lining up the entrance to give him a royal welcome, he entered the chairman's room with aplomb and sat down to do a puja.

At the press conference that followed, the entire newspaper fraternity of the city appeared to be present, not to mention many from outside too. The next day the press appeared to have been smitten with him, most papers giving him full-page coverage. Nobody could have imagined that a few years later he would lose the company and scoot to London.

———

Now, the complicated story of how the acquisition came about.

Manu Chhabria had acquired Shah Wallace in 1987 and thumbed his nose at India's liquor king. Mallya was very upset but could do little about what had happened. But opportunity soon presented itself, and in the most unexpected of ways.

When he flew back to Dubai after acquiring Shaw Wallace, Manu left behind his brother Kishore—nine years younger than him—to manage the Calcutta-based company. But very soon Manu started getting information—correct or incorrect, one does not know—that Kishore was dancing to his own number in the liquor company, running it in whatever fashion he wanted, and without keeping the elder brother informed. Not at all amused by this, Manu asked Kishore to move to Dunlop, another Calcutta-based company that he had acquired before Shah Wallace. But Kishore was not agreeable to this: he was enjoying himself at work in the liquor industry and learning the ropes fast. From this point onwards the differences between the two brothers began to grow, not the least because the relations between their wives were also not cordial. Sensing an opportunity to create mischief, company executives too started carrying tales about Kishore's doings or alleged doings in Shaw Wallace to Manu.

It was over a distillery company, BDA Ltd, that matters came to a head. This was a company Manu and Kishore's father and uncle had jointly taken over many years ago as it had a licence to manufacture liquor. Manu now asserted that BDA should be part of Shaw Wallace, but Kishore said the company ought to be his, citing a promise made to him earlier. Manu would not agree, and Kishore parted ways with his brother in 1992, suggesting that Manu was being very unhelpful and suspicious.

What is more, Kishore walked out taking BDA along and straightaway headed to embrace Vijay Mallya. He had reckoned that Mallya would be his friend because he was now an enemy of his enemy. The differences between the two brothers had escalated to such a level that they indeed began looking at each other as sworn enemies. Many years later, Kishore Chhabria said in an interview to P.G. Mathai of the

Telegraph: 'I was foolish enough to think that my enemy's enemy would be my friend. Manu had become my enemy and his enemy was Mallya.'

But this newfound friendship was not to last long—in fact, it added more complications to the situation. As part of his deal with Mallya, Kishore agreed to bring BDA into his fold. This would be effected by making BDA a subsidiary of the Mallya-held Herbertsons. Mallya wanted BDA because it produced the whisky Officer's Choice, the leader in its market segment. In return, for BDA, Kishore would be given half of Mallya's 55 per cent equity—27.5 per cent—in Herbertsons. Actually, Mallya wanted to offer Kishore shares in another outfit of his, Carew & Company, but Kishore insisted that he should get shares in Herbertsons. Mallya agreed. Kishore also was appointed the vice-chairman of Herbertsons.

There are two versions of what happened next. According to the Kishore version—as attributed to him in magazine and newspaper interviews, one of them being in the *Hindustan Times* of 7 December 2014—he was promised an active role in the management of Herbertsons as vice-chairman. But the moment he started asserting himself there, Mallya became quite upset. The story from the Mallya camp was that Kishore, with a foothold in Herbertsons, began buying more shares of the company in the name of some clandestine companies which just existed on paper. His objective was to gain control over Herbertsons, said Mallya's men. By doing this, Kishore also breached an 'agreement' that he had with Mallya. The 'agreement', which remained unsigned, specified that Kishore would not buy shares of Herbertsons from the market; and that if ever he sold his existing shares, the first right of refusal would be given to Mallya. Apparently, the 'agreement' was drawn up and the deal was done, but the signatures not appended to the document. This, of course, meant the 'agreement' could not be challenged in a court of law. Why the documents were not signed remains a mystery.

The Mallya camp also alleged that Kishore had bought shares in Herbertsons by siphoning off money from BDA, which by then was a subsidiary of Herbertsons. Moreover, he had bought such a large quantity of shares from the market that Mallya found himself reduced to a minority shareholder in Herbertsons.

Mallya manoeuvred to ensure that the shares Kishore had bought from the market were not registered in the books of the company, rendering the share purchases useless. Nonetheless, there was alarm in the Mallya camp, and legal proceedings were initiated against Kishore—in an indirect manner—to keep him in check. Mallya served a legal notice on Kishore, asking him to transfer the Officer's Choice brand from BDA to Herbertsons. This was something Kishore had been resisting all along. In 1995, Mallya had wanted Bombay Breweries, a facility that manufactured Kingfisher, to be transferred from Herbertsons Ltd to his own beer-making division.

But Kishore was smart too. He used his veto powers on the Herbertsons board to block this transfer. He insisted that the board first clear registration of 17 per cent of the shares that one of his companies had bought in Herbertsons before he could consider the transfer plea.

The battle of wits between Mallya and Kishore continued for some time. Their relationship became one of total mistrust. Mallya realized that Kishore had teamed up with him only as a stepping stone to build a liquor company of his own. Kishore wanted to demonstrate to his brother Manu that he too had business acumen. By 1998, Mallya sensed that Kishore, with his armoury of shares that he had acquired in Herbertsons, would soon mount a takeover bid on it. In an attempt to stop this, he first made himself the managing director of Herbertsons. This would give him more powers in running the company. Simultaneously, he also moved the Bombay High Court, securing an injunction that prevented Herbertsons from holding its annual general meeting and BDA from holding a meeting of its board of directors. Mallya was now empowered; a change of management could happen only after the shareholders voted in a general meeting. If there was no meeting of shareholders, Mallya could not be dislodged from the position of managing director at Herbertsons. A little later, he also moved the Company Law Board, complaining that Kishore had siphoned off money from BDA to buy shares of Herbertsons. A subsequent inquiry by the income tax department revealed mismanagement of funds in BDA.

All this made life a trifle difficult for Kishore during the closing years of the 1990s. As the screws tightened on him, he sued for peace. He offered to sell Mallya a stake of 49 per cent in Herbertsons. But this deal was not acceptable to the latter; in the first place, Kishore had acquired the shares illegally and now he demanded almost four times the price at which he had acquired them. What really got Mallya's goat was that Kishore also wanted BDA back as part of the deal. In 2001, the Bombay High Court ruled against Kishore, nullifying his acquisition of a 21 per cent stake in Herbertsons through market purchases.

While the fight between his younger brother Kishore and Mallya was raging, Manu passed away. At fifty-six, he was relatively young. Since he had no sons, his wife Vidya took over as chairperson of the Jumbo group that he ran. She also became the chairperson of Shaw Wallace. His three daughters—Kiran, Komal and Bhavita—demanded a role in the business too. Ultimately, Komal became the managing director of Shaw Wallace. But due to complex family relations and their lack of experience in running a big company, the mother and daughters agreed to sell off some of the businesses they held. They also decided to split Shaw Wallace Company into a spirits division and a beer division so that they could be sold off to two different suitors.

When news of this reached Mallya—indirectly, through market sources—he was very agitated. As described in Chapter 4, Chhabria had taken over Shaw Wallace using money from the company Carrasco, owned jointly by himself and Mallya. Mallya had denied to the Indian authorities that he had anything to do with this company, as admitting that he did would make him guilty of violating the Foreign Exchange Regulation Act (FERA). It was by citing this statement that Manu had denied Mallya half of Shaw Wallace. Mallya had filed a case relating to the ownership of Carrasco in a court in Hong Kong, where this company was incorporated. Like many court cases, this one too was hanging fire.

Now Mallya gave notice that he would sue the management of Shaw Wallace for trying to sell off the company before its ownership issue was disposed of by the Hong Kong court. If the court said that Mallya owned 50 per cent of Carrasco, then he would become part-owner of Shaw Wallace; the company could not be sold before the court ruled in the matter.

It so happened that Mallya's company McDowell owned a small stake in Shaw Wallace. This came in handy now, and Mallya, through McDowell, got a locus standi as an interested party to file a case seeking to restrain the Chhabrias from hiving off their assets, arguing that this would adversely affect 'minority shareholder interests'.

Mallya followed this up, first with a direct offer to the Chhabria family in late 2004 and then with an open offer to all shareholders of Shaw Wallace for taking over its liquor business. His direct offer consisted of a Rs 1,251 crore deal to buy up the spirits business. But sensing that this direct approach unsettled the family, he came up with an open offer to buy 25 per cent of Shaw Wallace Company, which he valued at Rs 350 crore.

At the same time, Mallya also moved the Bombay High Court to restrain SABMiller from entering into any deal with Shaw Wallace Company. He contended in his petition that this was to protect the interests of the Shaw Wallace shareholders. Industry observers saw this as a tactic to complicate matters for Manu's widow and daughters, to wear down their patience and push them to the brink.

In January 2004, the high court in Hong Kong ruled that Mallya was an equal partner in Carrasco, giving a twist to the whole matter. Immediately, the Jumbo group decided to challenge the order, arguing that this was in breach of Indian laws because at the time of Carrasco's incorporation no Indian company could own an overseas company without permission. Although the Jumbo group filed the case, Vidya was getting impatient: she realized that this battle would go on for years in various courts.

So she decided to respond to Mallya's overtures and settle

the dispute once and for all. He was very persuasive and camped in Dubai for a month. He refused to talk to anyone else in the company, sensing that she would be the most reasonable person at Shaw Wallace to deal with.

Before selling Shah Wallace's spirits division to Mallya, much paperwork had to be done. First, both parties had to file a consent form before the Hong Kong court that they had settled their differences. Upon this, the court dismissed the case before them.

Earlier, in 2003, Shaw Wallace had entered into a 50:50 deal with SABMiller, for which the latter was sold half of the equity of the beer division and its managerial control for $132.8 million. At that time, Shaw Wallace had twenty-two breweries producing 32 million cases annually. This accounted for 36 per cent of the entire beer market in India. Though Mallya had been earlier trying to foil this deal, he later showed understanding in letting it pass through. This had gone a long way in convincing Vidya that she could do business with him.

McDowell, through which Mallya did the deal, valued the spirits business of Shah Wallace at Rs 1,300 crore; going by this calculation, Mallya paid Rs 678 crore to Chhabria's family, which owned a 55 per cent stake in the company. Each share was valued at Rs 260. Separately, the family was paid Rs 169 crore as a non-compete fee for their assurance that they would not start another liquor company to compete with the business they had just sold. This took the total value of the deal to Rs 847 crore. The takeover brought into the Mallya stable three well-known whisky brands—the premium whisky Royal Challenge, the regular whisky Director's Special and the super-premium whisky Antiquity.

In a sense, Mallya had paid twice for the same asset: Shaw Wallace; the first time through his investment in Carrasco and the second time by paying the Chhabria family. The debatable question is why did he do so, especially as the Hong Kong court judgement in 2004 recognized that he was half owner of Carrasco? The simple answer is he realized that a foreign court order could not enforce his part ownership in a company incorporated in India. Trying to do so would open a Pandora's box of complications: the Chhabria family would ensure that he was enmeshed in myriad court cases that would block his acquisition of the coveted company.

Shaw Wallace brought with it twelve owned and eleven contracted distillers to Mallya's empire. Now he had twenty-seven owned and forty-eight contracted distillers. The total number of brands owned by the Mallya empire had now risen to 140 with the addition of sixty-five brands. The number of millionaire brands in his control went up to twelve.

Just a fortnight before he cut the deal with the Chhabria family, he also made up with Kishore—or so it appeared then. On 5 March 2005, the Supreme Court gave its nod to an out-of-court settlement between Mallya and Kishore. By this settlement, United Breweries was to acquire Kishore's entire 49.06 per cent stake in Herbertsons by paying Rs 131.16 crore. Kishore would also get back his company BDA that had in the interim become a subsidiary of Herbertsons. After the peace pipe was smoked, the two jointly moved the Bombay High Court to remove the seven-year injunction against Herbertsons holding an annual general meeting and BDA holding board meetings. Now, 92.21 per cent of the shares of Shaw Wallace were controlled directly or indirectly by Mallya outfits.

Shortly after both the deals were done, Ravi Nedungadi, the CFO and director, finance, of the UB Group told the press: 'The doors are now open for the consolidation of UB's spirit business and formation of United Spirits to synergise all its liquor business under one umbrella.' In fact, the formation of United Spirits was soon announced: this corporation would amalgamate four companies—McDowell, Herbertsons, Triumph Distillers and Vintners (TDV) and Shaw Wallace. The group now sold more than 60 million cases annually, Mallya's empire becoming the second largest distilleries conglomerate in the world. The coming together of the four companies—a mega merger—had the distinct potential of increased manufacturing efficiencies, greater cost efficiencies from joint packaging and transportation, as well as lower procurement costs.

Shaw Wallace's first annual general meeting with Mallya as the chairman took place in Kolkata on 21 September 2005, as mentioned earlier in the chapter. In the afternoon, after the meeting, he entered the office of Shaw Wallace on 4 Bankshall Street to a cheering crowd of thousands who had collected to witness the event. Overwhelmed by the welcome, Mallya said: 'This is an emotional moment for me.' He recorded his entry in a diary with a red pen the moment he sat at his desk in the chairman's office.

———

Mallya had victoriously entered Shaw Wallace but the spat between him and Kishore was yet to conclude. There were more twists and turns, and to all appearances they were on account of Mallya's doings.

Although the Chhabria brothers had bitterly fought with each other through the 1990s, there were signs of a thaw as the decade came to a close. They began to meet again, although they would argue fiercely for hours together behind closed doors. But for lunch they would break bread together—perhaps blood *is* thicker than water. In 2001, the brothers decided to withdraw all the legal cases they had filed against each other. They numbered a grand 140. However, for some strange reason, Manu did not withdraw one case. This came back to haunt Kishore after Manu's death because Mallya used it against him to the hilt. In this case of 1992, Shaw Wallace had demanded the return of BDA along with the Officer's Choice whisky brand to it by Kishore.

After his 2005 deal with Kishore settling their dispute and handing BDA back to Kishore, Mallya revived this case in the Calcutta High Court. He contended that by virtue of acquiring Shaw Wallace he had also inherited the cases filed by the company. By implication, what had been demanded by the old management (Manu Chhabria) of Shaw Wallace would have to be continued by the new management (Vijay Mallya). Thus began a new battle; Mallya now sought what he had just handed over to Kishore. However, the Mallya camp squarely blamed Kishore for catalysing discord once again. They alleged that in 2006, a designate of Kishore's had showed up at the court-convened extraordinary general meeting (EGM) of Herbertsons and opposed Mallya's plans to consolidate the company into United Spirits. This incensed Mallya, who felt Kishore was still not allowing him to go about his business in peace.

The dispute was resolved—once again, out of court—in early October 2012. The resolution, ratified by the Calcutta

High Court, provided for Officer's Choice whisky to remain with Kishore and directed that his company, Allied Blenders' and Distillers (ABD), pay Rs 8 crore to United Spirits Limited (USL) towards withdrawal of court cases claiming their right on Officer's Choice whisky. But this time Mallya was in a hurry to settle the dispute. He was by now neck deep in trouble brought on by the collapse of Kingfisher Airlines and desperately needed cash. For this reason he had also made up his mind to sell part of United Spirits to the largest liquor manufacturer of the world, Diageo. Mallya required a hassle-free environment to ensure that the deal could proceed smoothly. A legal case still hanging could prove disruptive. Mallya now moved in earnest to resolve the long-standing dispute lest it should cast its shadow on the Diageo deal.

8

Mallya's Foray into Politics

RAMAKRISHNA HEGDE WAS THE chief minister of Karnataka when Vijay Mallya took over the reins at the UB Group in late 1983. Mallya knew that for presiding efficiently over a liquor business, he would need to maintain good relations with the government. It was essential for liquor manufacturers to be on the right side of the powers-that-be, as liquor was still considered a none-too-respectable business in the mid-1980s. With this in mind, Mallya started cultivating the chief minister.

Born in 1926, Hegde was a man of Mallya's father's age, twenty-eight years older than him. But this huge age difference did not come in the way of a close bond developing between the two. They had much in common: in the world of politics dominated by many rustic actors, Hegde was not a run-of-the-mill politician. He had a personality of his own and was engaged in activities like theatre. In this respect he was much like Mallya, who, while being a businessman, had varied interests. To add to this, both were from the same region—north Canara (now called the Uttara Kannada district).

Over the years, their relationship matured. One day Hegde

told Mallya that he must join politics, suggesting that he could be his political successor. By that time Hegde was no longer the chief minister, having been edged out by caste politics in the state. There were (and still are) two politically dominant castes in Karnataka—the Lingayats and the Vokkaligas; the path to the Vidhana Soudha in Bangalore is controlled by them. Sometimes a balance between the two communities can be established by an outsider, and it was in such a situation that Hegde had become the chief minister. He was a Brahmin. Brahmins were a numerically small community, not feared by Karnataka's dominant castes yet respected for their tradition of learning. Mallya was also a Brahmin, and Hegde suggested to his protégé that he must use this to muscle his way to power. Another consideration, of course, was that Mallya had money.

An interesting feature of Karnataka politics is that between 1980 and 2004, 'liquor money' had played a big role in funding it. The liquor lobby was obviously very powerful. It began with arrack, but a few years down the line IMFL manufacturers ruled the roost. In all fairness, it was not UB but another company that played a dominant role in this game. If political analysts are to be believed, a central feature of state politics in those days was widespread excise evasion by liquor manufacturers in cahoots with the ruling party. As a result, a huge amount of liquor was overlooked by the excise department, robbing the state of revenues.

The liquor on which revenues were not paid was referred to as 'seconds', but was sold in the market at the prevailing prices. As can be guessed, the illegal profits were shared between the liquor manufacturers and their political patrons. This continued until 2004, when Chief Minister S.M. Krishna of the Congress took liquor distribution into the state's hands. If liquor had to be distributed through state-owned corporations, then tax could not be evaded. Thus the liquor lobby was cut down to size—only to yield way to other lobbies, though, such as education, real estate and mining.

By 2002, Mallya was a Member of Parliament, having been elected to the Rajya Sabha with the support of the Janata Dal (United) and Janata Dal (Secular) parties. JD(S) was the party of H.D. Deve Gowda, who had been prime minister between June 1996 and April 1997. JD(U) had aligned with the BJP and was part of the NDA government that ruled India from 1998 to 2004. But on 10 August 2002, Mallya joined JD(U) and was immediately appointed as the vice-president of the party. While joining the party, he announced that he was doing so on the advice of Ramakrishna Hegde. 'I have publicly stated that my father figure and mentor is Mr Hegde. He is largely instrumental in getting me into Parliament. Following his advice and wishes, I am joining JD (U),' he said. He polled fifty-one votes against the requirement of forty-five in the polls that took place for the post.

He became an MP in only his second attempt. In 2000, he had contested for the Rajya Sabha but lost. He had contested as an independent candidate and had expected to win by getting votes across the board. But the Congress party made it a point to vote against him and put up three candidates of its own. He had good relations with Krishna, whose daughter was married to his step-brother, and this was the reason for his optimism. But the Congress high command had ordered that Mallya should be defeated at any cost because he was closely connected with Hegde, a decidedly anti-Congress person. On the night before the polls, Krishna hosted a dinner

An ad for Kingfisher beer in Goa. Kingfisher beer, a globally known brand, had made Vijay Mallya the largest manufacturer and distributor of beer in India.

The tailfin of a Kingfisher Airlines Airbus A330-200. The original Kingfisher logo was black and white and depicted the bird in a sitting position. Mallya had colour added and the bird shown in flight to convey dynamism and energy.

Siddharth Mallya at a GQ Men of the Year Awards event in 2011. Mallya's only son, Siddharth has little interest in his father's business and wants to make it big as an actor and model. *Getty Images*

Actor Deepika Padukone at a Kingfisher Calendar Girl event in 2011. The Kingfisher swimsuit calendar, which launched Padukone, was an institution of sorts in itself. *Getty Images*

Actor John Abraham and Vijay Mallya unveil the Kingfisher Swimsuit Special Calendar 2008 in Mumbai on 9 December 2007. *Getty Images*

Alfonso Celis (left) of Mexico, Sergio Perez (second from left) of Mexico and Esteban Ocon (right) of France pose with Vijay Mallya and the VJM10 car during the Sahara Force India Formula One team launch at Silverstone on 22 February 2017 in Northampton, England. The Spyker F1 team was renamed as Force India in 2007 after Mallya bought it. It later became Sahara Force India after the Sahara group purchased 42 per cent of its shares. *Getty Images*

Mallya's superyacht, *Indian Empress*, in the Grand Harbour as seen from Valletta in Vittoriosa, Malta, on 29 March 2017. According to a report in *Mumbai Mirror* in May 2013, Mallya's girlfriend Pinky Lalwani was introduced to him at the annual billionaires' party on the occasion of the Monaco Grand Prix weekend held on the superyacht.
Getty Images

Mallya with Royal Challengers Bangalore captain Rahul Dravid and other members during the launch of the IPL team in Bangalore on 12 March 2008. When the auction for IPL teams was conducted in January that year, Mallya bid Rs 440 crore, marginally less than Mukesh Ambani's bid of Rs 441 crore, and bagged a team for Bangalore. *Getty Images*

Cheerleaders at an RCB match in 2009. In IPL's first edition, Mallya had hired a twelve-member cheerleading squad that Washington Redskins used to requisition for the US National Football League. Their skimpy dresses had raised the hackles of Hindutva activists. *Getty Images*

A view of Mallya's UB City in 2010. Mallya opened up his prime estate in the heart of Bangalore to build UB City, billed to be the city's biggest commercial property, in 2004. Planned on 13 acres of land, UB City would carry 93,000 square metres of high-end commercial, retail and service apartment space.

Mallya in a royal horse carriage on his way to the race track for the Kingfisher Ultra Indian Derby, with prize money of Rs 2 crore, in 2016 in Mumbai. The derby attracted the best jockeys and the finest horses from across the world.

An inside view of Mallya's personal aircraft, an Airbus A319-133, which contained, among other expensive artifacts, a Picasso original. The plane was put up for auction by the service tax department in November 2016 in a bid to recover Mallya's dues.

for Congress legislators to keep the flock together. Mallya managed only thirty-five votes, well short of the required forty-five.

After he got elected to the Rajya Sabha in his second attempt, Bangalore journalist Asha Rai wrote in the *Economic Times*: 'Now that getting into Parliament has been accomplished—if the grapevine in town has to be believed—at great expense, would he be eyeing a ministerial berth?' Rai also noted in the same piece: 'Even people close to him are pretty surprised by his almost childlike enthusiasm for the job.' Soon after he got elected, Mallya faced a petition in Karnataka High Court challenging his election. The petitioner, D.K. Thara Devi, who had lost the polls, argued that Mallya was a non-resident Indian (NRI) and did not owe allegiance to India; on this ground his election should be declared null and void. But the high court bought Mallya's argument that he was ordinarily a resident of Bangalore and that his NRI status was only for the purpose of ease of effecting investments abroad. Moreover, he was assessed for income tax in India in Kolkata and was not a citizen of any other country.

Mallya was not destined to remain in the JD(U) for long. Fuelled by his ambition to become the main challenger to the ruling Congress party in Karnataka, he tried to work towards merging the JD(U) and JD(S). But his own party men foiled his attempts.

'They did not like my appointment as vice-president. If they did not like it they should have told Mr Hegde,' Mallya said a few months later. 'There were too many people with their own agenda in the party, and all the time they were trying to pull me down. Nobody likes my strong stand and firm decisions.'

Ultimately, on 14 April 2003, Mallya left the party and joined the Janata Party (JP). This was the original JP formed in 1977 after the Emergency. In Election Commission parlance, it had become an unrecognized but registered party. JD(S) and JD(U) had emerged from the JP, but JP's party symbol was now with the maverick politician Subramanian Swamy. On the advice of Hegde, Mallya joined the JP and was straightaway appointed as its national working president. 'We are going to rekindle the past spirit of the Janata Party. I am going to work in all states,' Mallya announced after taking over as the national president. Swamy and Hegde had had great differences until then, but Mallya claimed he had brought about a patch-up with Swamy.

The ambitious Mallya decided that his party must make a bid for power in the 2004 Lok Sabha elections. 'Mallya was attending Rajya Sabha sessions, and the impression that he got was that many MPs had no clue how the economy worked. So the debates often did not reflect practical solutions. As a businessman, he felt he had the proper approach to get work done,' says a Mallya camp follower. Mallya also felt the government was not cashing in on the entrepreneurial spirit of the people and was relying on consumer aspirations to boost demand, and through that also boost growth rates in the country. It seems that Mallya was highly influenced by Ross Perot, the American businessman who ran for president twice, in 1992 and 1996, and performed creditably. Silvio Berlusconi, the business tycoon who became the prime minister of Italy, was another inspiration for Mallya. (The many scandals relating to Berlusconi surfaced much later).

He also energetically participated in the Karnataka assembly elections in 2004. He wanted to put up candidates for all 224 seats in the state, but could find only 155 'winnable' candidates. He even survived an air crash on his campaign flight to Bagalkot from Hubli. Luckily, he escaped with minor injuries and resumed his campaigning very soon. But the results of the elections were disastrous for him. The Janata Party could not win a single seat. Worse still, 153 of his 155 candidates lost their deposits. The party won just 2.01 per cent of all the votes polled!

His six Janata Party candidates put up for the 2004 Lok Sabha elections also lost, all having to relinquish their deposits. They polled only 0.63 per cent of the total vote. The ambitious Mallya had even extended Janata Party activities to cover states like Andhra Pradesh, Orissa (now Odisha) and West Bengal, all in vain.

'He also used his Mercedes-Benz to electioneer. People turned up at his meetings more to see this man who was known to surround himself with pretty women in skimpy bikinis. To their horror, they found well-dressed UB executives with him,' Srinivasa Prasad, then political bureau chief of the *Times of India* in Bangalore, later wrote in FirstPost on 15 March 2016.

Obviously, Mallya's optimism was unrealistic and not matched by ground realities. 'You cannot run a political party as a beer party,' a wag had noted after Mallya's debacle. In January 2004, Hegde had died after a prolonged illness and wasn't around to caution Mallya against his foolish misadventures. How much money he lost in the elections is not known, but it must have been quite substantial.

The party may have been wrecked but his personal political ambitions were intact. Incidentally, he made a special effort to appeal to the minority voters in the polls. Just a fortnight before the first phase of the state polls, he called for a press conference and displayed the sword of Tipu Sultan, which had been seized by British officers after the siege of Seringapatam on 4 May 1799. Tipu, known as the Tiger of Mysore, had died in the battle, and the English soldiers had taken his sword away to England.

In September 2003, the sword was auctioned in London by the family of the English army officer who had taken possession of it. It was bought by a mysterious buyer at a price equivalent of Rs 1.5 crore. Mallya revealed at a press conference that he was the mysterious buyer of the forty-two-inch-long sword, with its gold loop and scabbard of velvet with silver gilt. He said he had purchased it with his personal wealth to restore the 'pride of Karnataka'. He vehemently denied any political motive behind his new acquisition though few were willing to believe him.

At the press conference, he had on the dais the traditional guardians of the *dargah* of Khwaja Garib Nawaz in Ajmer. The industrialist-turned-politician said that he had sought the blessings of the Sufi saint before entering politics.

Although Tipu Sultan had fought against the British, he is not held in high esteem by the Hindus in Karnataka, who consider him a bigot. But Tipu enjoys a great reputation among the Muslims and among a small section of Hindus in the state. Mallya was flogging the icon to attract the Muslim vote, but his strategy did not work.

Being part of the power establishment gives a different sort of kick to businessmen. It was no different with Mallya. He had made new friends and contacts. Being an MP gave him a different type of clout in the corridors of power in

Delhi—something an ordinary businessman could not aspire to. No minister or bureaucrat could take him lightly. In fact, he became friends with some of them. For Mallya, contacts had become even more important, now that he had embarked on running an airline. Journalists covering the Parliament beat noted that many MPs also warmed up to him, expecting goodies from him, including invites to his fabulous parties on his private yacht and rides on his personal plane. Mallya was also known for gifting whiskies to MPs once a year.

———

During his Rajya Sabha tenure, the political landscape of Karnataka underwent a change. When Mallya's term came to an end in April 2008, the state was poised for an election and did not have a legislative assembly (whose members comprise the voters who elect a Rajya Sabha MP). Voting was postponed, pending elections to the legislative assembly. Mallya, however, was impatient. He could not wait. He began talking to the bosses of the Shiv Sena to see if they could send him to the Rajya Sabha from Maharashtra. But the talks failed as the Shiv Sena told Mallya they were not in favour of giving a ticket to a non-Maharashtrian. (This was not strictly correct because in the past they had given a ticket to journalist-turned-filmmaker Pritish Nandy).

When the legislative assembly was in place in Karnataka in June 2008, Mallya found it difficult to swing a deal for himself. One of the candidates for the Rajya Sabha was the former chief minister, S.M. Krishna himself. Another candidate controlled hundreds of colleges in Karnataka and a dozen abroad, and could therefore be very resourceful. Realizing he would come a cropper, Mallya did not contest the election and reconciled himself to his fate.

But his sights remained on the Rajya Sabha, and two years later, when the elections were held again (elections for the upper house of Parliament are held biennially), he was back, lobbying for a seat for himself.

In 2009, he had bought some personal effects of Mahatma Gandhi that were auctioned in New York. The effects included Gandhiji's glasses, his sandals, pocket watch, a plate and a bowl. The Government of India was appalled at such an auction and demanded that these private properties of the Father of the Nation be given back to India. But the auctioneers did not relent. Mallya then 'bid for the country', buying the effects for $1.8 million (Rs 9.3 crore). This did much to enhance his stature in India. There were many, of course, who thought this was yet another move on his part to gain popularity in his quest for a Rajya Sabha seat.

Mallya had done his homework well this time and made it up with the JD(S), the party led by Deve Gowda and his son H.D. Kumaraswamy. When Kumaraswamy was the chief minister in 2006, Mallya had gone hammer and tongs at him, accusing him of 'raising objections about every possible infrastructure project'. But now, four years later, the two were so friendly that Kumaraswamy was by Mallya's side when he filed his nomination papers!

The JD(S) had decided to support Mallya but did not have the numbers to guarantee his win. He was now dependent on five independents and the surplus votes of the BJP. But when the press asked him if he was confident of a win, he shot back: 'If I wasn't confident of winning, I wouldn't have filed nomination papers. I will work out a strategy with H.D. Kumaraswamy.' The moment Mallya had filed his papers, Swamy sacked him for 'accepting the nomination of JD(S)'. Swami also accused him of failure to function effectively as the working president of the Janata Party and remarked that anyway 'his appointment was on an ad hoc basis'.

But the strategy that Mallya worked out with the JD(S) bosses was successful, and on 1 July 2010 he was back in the Rajya Sabha for a second term. This term would have continued till 30 June 2016, but in early May 2016 Mallya submitted his resignation after realizing that the ethics committee of the Rajya Sabha would recommend his axing from the upper house, as mentioned earlier. Obviously, he preferred to quit rather than be sacked. His first resignation letter did not bear his signature and was rejected. Although his second resignation letter came after the ethics committee had recommended his sacking, Vice President Hamid Ansari, who is also the chairman of the Rajya Sabha, saved Mallya the blushes and accepted his resignation.

———

Soon after he was first elected to the Rajya Sabha in 2002, a bunch of Bangaloreans had petitioned Mallya, asking for the bars in the city to be allowed to remain open till 2 a.m. 'I do not mix business with politics,' he had declared. But one of the first questions he had asked in the Rajya Sabha had pertained to levies by different states on liquor and customs duties on imported foreign liquor. He had raised a question on 16 July 2002, asking the Union finance minister whether the reduction of additional customs duty on foreign liquor in the previous budget would not encourage import of cheap liquor into the country. He also sought to know the justification for import of liquor 'in view of constitutional provisions and various restrictions imposed on the domestic industry'.

But soon afterwards his questions relating to his business interests ceased and he turned his attention to problems faced by Karnataka. Over his two terms in the upper house, he asked many questions on many matters, including construction of the second phase of the metro in Bangalore, radiation from mobile towers, high-speed rail links between Mysore and Bangalore, declaration of classical status for the Kannada language, construction of sports complexes in every taluka of Karnataka, coal linkage to power plants and hostels for girl students from the Other Backward Classes (OBC). He never initiated any private member's bill, nor did he raise any call attention motion. Curiously, he asked many questions relating to airports in Karnataka. However, Parliament watchers say he was not at all prolific in raising questions. In fact, his questions were barely half the average number for an MP. He was not known to have participated in many debates in the house either.

Mallya was a member of the consultative committee of MPs for the civil aviation ministry from August 2010 onwards. This is significant, because his appointment to the committee came at precisely the same time when Kingfisher's travails began. Being on the committee gave him an unfair advantage vis-à-vis his competition. 'It was most unfair to us. By virtue of his membership of this committee, he became part of the policy-making circles of civil aviation and knew what the thinking of the government was on various issues. He also was able to use his privileged position to influence

government on matters concerning Kingfisher Airlines,' says a
senior official at Air India who did not want to be identified.
When he left the Rajya Sabha, Mallya was a member of
the commerce committee. At different points during his
tenure he had been a member of consultative committees of
various ministries, such as defence production, science and
technology, and industry.

Mallya's attendance in Parliament was a low 30 per
cent—not very different from the record of many other MPs.
However, his presence in the Parliament building attracted
attention because he arrived in stylish cars; sometimes he
drove up in his Maserati, which had a powerful three-litre
engine that could take it to a speed of up to 290 km per hour.
He was also very elegantly dressed.

Other than powering himself up to be an MP, he also
bought into an English national daily, the *Asian Age*, to
build a positive image for himself. As mentioned earlier, he
first picked up the franchise for the Bangalore edition of the
paper, later buying up the Calcutta edition in 1998. He went
on to become the major shareholder in the paper itself, with
its multiple editions, including a New Delhi one. He remained
the majority owner for many years (before divesting from it
in the wake of trouble at Kingfisher). 'Many industrialists
these days think that owning a newspaper comes in handy,
not only for building a positive image but also for furthering
their political interests. Further, it can be used to counter
stories against them,' says a leading image consultant.

Mallya also maintained close relations with liquor
businessmen-turned-politicians, whom he cultivated to
further his interests. A good example was D.K. Audikesavulu
Naidu, better known as DKA, a distiller-turned-MP whose

sway straddled the four southern states and many political parties like the Congress and the Telugu Desam Party. DKA began brewing beer for United Breweries and set up a huge plant exclusively for Mallya's company. He was also the main distributor of his IMFL in Karnataka for a few years. Introduced to Mallya by Hegde, DKA at one time also held the powerful post of chairman of the Tirupati Tirumala Devasthanam (TTD). As a Congressman, he was charged with bribing MPs in the Jharkhand Mukti Morcha (JMM) case to save the Narasimha Rao government in the early 1990s. In 2008, as a TDP MP, he defied the party whip and voted for the Manmohan Singh government in the no-confidence motion against it. Those in the know say that DKA—who died in April 2013—acted as a troubleshooter for Mallya in many matters.

Another close associate of Mallya's has been Magunta Sreenivasulu Reddy, who has been a member of the Lok Sabha for three terms. Chairman of the Balaji group, Reddy has many businesses, including liquor. Mallya and Reddy are so close that the latter also serves on the board of UB Engineering. When Mangalore Chemicals & Fertilizers was part of the Mallya empire, Reddy was on the board of this company too. It is believed that in times of financial distress at UB—which had been overstretched in the Kingfisher crisis—Reddy had extended loans to Mallya.

As Mallya's conviction in a cheque-bouncing case made news in April 2016, a Right to Information (RTI) request was made by a public-spirited individual to the Rajya Sabha Secretariat to find out how regular Mallya was in claiming all the allowances he was entitled to. The replies showed that Mallya had claimed most of the allowances he was entitled to; of course, there was nothing out of order in his doing so. He claimed his salary of Rs 50,000 per month and his constituency allowance (Rs 20,000 a month in the beginning, and later Rs 45,000 a month). He also claimed a secretarial allowance of Rs 6,000 per month (in the middle of his term, this was raised to Rs 15,000 per month). The RTI reply also revealed that Mallya had raised a bill of Rs 1.73 lakh for calls made from his official phone number. He, however, did not claim his water, electricity or medical expenses. Neither did he claim any reimbursement for travelling by air.

Summarizing his political activities, it appears that Mallya made full use of his position to get close to the powers-that-be, subtly though this was done. His position as a public representative opened for him many doors to the corridors of power.

9

Sporting Ventures

CASHING IN ON THE enormous popularity of cricket in the Indian subcontinent, the Zee TV group founded the Indian Cricket League (ICL) in 2007. Teams from India, Pakistan and Bangladesh, along with a World XI team, began participating in the T20 cricket tournament, much to the chagrin of the Board of Control for Cricket in India (BCCI). The BCCI was alarmed to realize that its monopoly over the game was being seriously challenged. With the support of the International Cricket Council (ICC), it banned for lifetime those cricketers who participated in the ICL. At the same time it tasked a smart businessman, Lalit Modi—also its vice-president—with the job of developing an alternative to the ICL.

The very next year, in 2008, Modi was ready with his model. This was the Indian Premier League (IPL), which would have eight participating teams, one each from Delhi, Mumbai, Kolkata, Bangalore, Chennai, Hyderabad, Chandigarh and Jaipur. The team for each city would be auctioned to the highest bidder. The winning bidders would then buy players for their team through an auction. The game would be on the lines of the T20 model, beginning in the evening and stretching into the night, drawing a large numbers of spectators, both live and on television. The IPL season was fixed for the summer months; it was in essence a summer carnival, designed to get corporations to promote, advertise or market their products on the field or through television commercials.

Many top businessmen found the IPL idea exciting, and this included Vijay Mallya. The liquor baron realized that the IPL presented a great opportunity for advertising his liquor, an item not allowed to be advertised. It was an avenue for image building and networking. And possession of a team would also give its owner 'unlimited bragging rights' (as some wags commented).

This was not the first time that Mallya had entered the world of cricket. Around 1995, when one-day internationals and the World Cup tournament were at the peak of their popularity, Vijay wanted to brand the West Indies cricket team. In his estimation, the Caribbean team was not only the best in the world but also the most fun-loving. They represented just the same values that his Kingfisher brand did. The West Indies Cricket Board, however, lacked one thing: it did not have enough money to strengthen its team and empower it for the long run. Mallya proposed to the board that he would sponsor the team, but in return wanted it to be renamed as the Kingfisher West Indies team.

The board was game but there was enormous public resentment. This was not surprising because cricket represented the cultural pride of the West Indies, a conglomeration of small erstwhile colonized nations that did not have much else going for it.

The West Indies press started protesting that the national

pride and the family silver were being bartered away. The Barbados prime minister also criticized the proposal. Faced with so much opposition, the West Indies Cricket Board called off the decision to brand its team. Kingfisher's sponsorship of the team, however, continued.

Incidentally, the lyrics 'Ula la la la le yo' that became famous very soon, were composed at this time. Barbados was to reappear in Mallya's cricket plans once again—in 2016, just before he scooted from India. In fact, it related to the last acquisition he made before exiting the country—more on that later in the chapter.

When the auction for the IPL was conducted on 24 January 2008, Mallya bid Rs 440 crore, marginally less than Mukesh Ambani's bid of Rs 441 crore. The top eight bidders in the auction were allowed their choice of city, provided they had specifically bid for that city. Mukesh chose Mumbai, much to Mallya's discomfiture. He too had coveted Mumbai—after all, the city was the largest in the country. He then opted for Bangalore, which anyway was his home turf. After landing a team, he told media persons: 'I am delighted that the UB Group has won a team. We will now use this as an active promotional platform for all our brands.'

The buyers could name their own teams and even list them on the stock market if they wished to. Mallya toyed with the idea of naming his team after McDowell's No. 1, his highest-selling whisky, but ultimately decided to name it after another of his whisky brands, Royal Challenge. The team was named Royal Challengers Bangalore (RCB). However, not all the winning bidders named their team after the brands they sold.

Ambani's team was called Mumbai Indians and the GMR group's team in Delhi, the Delhi Daredevils. But Mallya was very clear about what he wanted to do with his team. He understood branding very well and had been a master of the game ever since he stepped into his father's shoes in 1983.

Very soon a logo was designed for the team: it said 'Royal Challengers' in yellow, embossed in a red circle (the yellow would be replaced by gold the next year). At the top of the emblem was a crown bearing the figure of a roaring lion. A theme song was also composed for the team: '*Jeetenge hum shaan se*' (We will win in style). Four brand ambassadors from the film world were appointed for the team: Katrina Kaif, Deepika Padukone, Ramya and Upendra. The last two were regional film stars from the Kannada movie industry. As if all this was not enough, Mallya hired the twelve-member cheerleading squad that Washington Redskins used to requisition for the US National Football League. The squad's job was to fire up the players and get the crowds cheering, but the skimpy dresses they wore raised the hackles of Hindutva activists, forcing the cheerleaders to wear dresses that covered them fully.

South Africa's Jacques Kallis became the most expensive player bought by RCB, at $900,000. Rahul Dravid was named the icon player of the team—an icon player got 15 per cent more than the highest paid player in the team. Mallya also recruited the then Indian cricket team captain Anil Kumble for RCB.

The success of Mallya's liquor business lay in his delegation of power to excellent managers who understood their business very well. Running an IPL cricket team was also a full-time affair that required excellent managers. Mallya had built his liquor team over time and with experience. He could not do this in cricket. And with Kingfisher Airlines flying high, he had no time to devote to the operations of his cricket team. A chief executive officer and manager, Charu Sharma, was appointed. So was a coach—former Indian pacer Venkatesh Prasad. Along with Dravid, these two recruits ran the affairs of the team.

But the team performed very poorly. In the inaugural season it won four matches but lost ten. RCB stood second from the bottom. Mallya was extremely displeased and expressed his unhappiness even as the league matches were on. He publicly criticized both Sharma and Dravid for not choosing the team properly. He also confessed that he should have been more involved personally. Apparently, he had made some suggestions about who should be on the team but Sharma had ignored them. His anger towards Sharma mounted as he also began to believe that Sharma could not get his players to bond well and had not set up good practice facilities for them. Not surprising then that Sharma was sacked midway through the series and former Indian player and Bangalorean Brijesh Patel appointed in his place. Another dampener for Vijay was that Kallis had to be put on the bench midway through the tournament, having performed poorly.

RCB emerged as the only team that tried eleven opening combinations in fourteen matches. At the end of the season, its chief cricketing officer, Martin Crowe, resigned.

———

In the next season in 2009, Mallya personally took charge. After the humiliating defeat of his team the year before, the theme song was changed to a less ambitious 'Game for more'.

Kevin Pietersen, valued at $1.5 million, was hired by RCB.

Mallya announced that the captaincy of the team had been kept open and that the team management would take a call on it later. The team started with Dravid as captain, but mid-tournament Mallya announced that Pietersen would replace him, as Dravid was supposedly grappling with family-related problems. But that was not the end of the story.

Pietersen soon left to play for England against the West Indies in a test series. Now, Kumble became the captain of the team, and under him RCB did very well, steadily moving forward. It ultimately landed up in the finals, which it lost by six runs to Deccan Chargers, the team from Hyderabad.

In the 2010 season, RCB was not very active in acquiring players—not surprising, considering that Mallya was running up huge debts because of Kingfisher Airlines. Ultimately, the team emerged third in the season.

In 2011, Daniel Vettori, a former New Zealand captain, was hired for $550,000. The team lost three matches at the outset of the tournament. Chris Gayle was brought mid-tournament. The team had Virat Kohli too, but in those days he was not the star that he later became. RCB went on to do well that year, reaching the finals, but again losing, this time to Chennai Super Kings.

In 2012—a bad year for Mallya's business, marked by Kingfisher's grounding—RCB brought on board Australian all-rounder Andrew Macdonald from Delhi Daredevils, paying a transfer fee of $100,000 for him. Muttiah Muralitharan of Sri Lanka was bought for $220,000 at the players' auction. The season started with an injured Chris Gayle. Team performance was also poor, though not purely on account of Gayle's injury. RCB failed to enter the champion's league, to which teams that had performed well in the league stage graduated.

In 2014, the team did not fare much better. This was its first year with Virat Kohli as captain. Gayle continued on the team. In 2015, when Kohli continued to be its captain and Gayle too was on the team, RCB ended up as semi-finalists, losing to Chennai Super Kings.

Revenues from cricket were measly, and in this business Mallya ran losses. Financial data is not easy to come by, but the *Mint* reported on 10 November 2014 that RCB had made losses of Rs 5.42 crore in 2010-11, Rs 7.07 crore in 2011-12 and Rs 7.85 crore in 2012-13. This was not surprising, considering that the money an IPL franchisee makes depends much on its team's performance. About 60 to 70 per cent of an IPL franchisee's revenues come from 'media rights'.

This revenue is collected by the BCCI (which manages the IPL) from parties who buy the rights to telecast the matches. The BCCI keeps 20 per cent of the revenues for itself, and after subtracting 8 per cent for the prize money, distributes the remaining 72 per cent among the teams. The teams receive money in proportion to their overall ranking at the end of the season, the logic being that the team with a high ranking has played more matches, is seen more on TV and has fetched higher viewership.

RCB's performance being patchy, the team did not earn much from this reward system. Although many of the IPL teams reported profits—most by keeping a tight leash on finances—analysts believe it is unlikely that a franchisee can make a profit in the short run. The team owner's investment is for the long run, they say. With his other businesses sinking,

Mallya had little financial stamina left to concentrate on RCB, and in 2016 stepped down from his ownership of the team.

———

It's a different matter that Mallya had had long experience in managing sporting teams. Kolkata is home to some of the best clubs in Indian football, many of them competing fiercely against each other. The rivalry extends to their large groups of supporters and fans, who are almost fanatical in their allegiance to their teams. The best-known football teams in the city are Mohun Bagan and East Bengal. Roughly speaking, their supporters are from the western and eastern parts respectively of undivided Bengal.

Though football is played with passion in Bengal, patronage for the state's football teams declined as trade and commerce receded from Bengal after 1970. This was a pity, because the rise of Kolkata's oldest football club, Mohun Bagan, is linked with the rise of Indian and Bengali nationalism. Mohun Bagan was founded by Bhupendra Nath Basu in 1889, and the game began to attract the hoi polloi. The entire team of Mohun Bagan played barefoot, a sign of how popular the game was even in the mofussil areas of the state.

In 1911, at the height of the Bengal Partition protest movement (against the arbitrary division of Bengal into East and West Bengal as part of the British plan of balkanization), the club had a major victory in a football match which did much to boost the Bengali and anti-British sentiment. It lifted the Indian Football Association (IFA) Shield, beating the East Yorkshire Regiment team. The well-built soldiers of the Yorkshire regiment playing with shoes were out-dribbled by the barefoot Bengali team in a match that became part of Bengal's folklore. Though not a native Bengali, Mallya, brought up in Calcutta, picked up the legends of the city. What bothered him was that Calcutta, with its hoary football ancestry, appeared nowhere in the international circuit. In fact, this was true not only of Calcutta but also of India. The Indian team could not compete in the Asian Cup, and one could not even imagine its participation in the World Cup. That the standard of football was so low in the country in spite of its having an All India Football Federation (AIFF) made Mallya wonder whether corporatization of Indian football clubs might not be the only way forward to professionalize them. This, of course, suited his business interests too.

The 1998-99 season was an epic year for Kolkata's football clubs. Mallya entered into deals with both the leading football teams of the city—Mohun Bagan and East Bengal. The deal was simple: the clubs were converted into companies, and Mallya, through United Breweries, bought 50 per cent each of their equity. He inducted five directors into each of the companies from UB, and another five directors into each from the respective clubs. Mallya himself became the chairman of both the companies. A huge sum of money was also pumped into the clubs, which were in a financially precarious state. In fact, $2 million was pumped into Mohun Bagan.

Of course, Mallya pushed in his commercial interests by renaming the companies McDowell Mohun Bagan and Kingfisher East Bengal. The players of the two football teams wore jerseys emblazoned with Mallya's brand logos. The arrangement of owning two rival companies, though not illegal, was not in the fitness of things. But the chieftains of the two teams had been sold a dream—that their teams would achieve international standards, bringing glory at home and abroad. There would be a football academy, a junior team and a club house. The standards of football would go up and the clubs would become like international football clubs, acquiring huge influence and clout. It was this dream and the lure of lucre that got the club chieftains to agree to Mallya's plan. An earlier attempt, in 1996, by the clubs themselves to professionalize their entire set-up through the intervention of the AIFF had failed.

This was because the AIFF was in a state of hibernation; nothing would stir it to action, not even petitions by football clubs requesting transparency in drafting professional guidelines for sponsorship, assignment of TV rights, and regulations for swapping of players between clubs. Finding that the AIFF was dragging its feet, Mallya set up an Indian Premier Football Association (IPFA), and this finally stirred the sleeping giant awake. But the new transparency measures adopted in 1996 did not work. There was too much mismanagement within the clubs. This was when Mallya realized that he could have a say if only he bought the leading teams!

With the two teams in his pocket, Mallya now tried to buy the third most important football team in Kolkata. Mohammedan Sporting had lost a bit of its sting after Partition but none of its pride. The club would not allow the team name to be prefixed with the name of a Mallya company product, and this put paid to Mallya's plans. In fact, there was trouble with Mohun Bagan too because some members of the club had opposed the deal with United Breweries and had moved the Calcutta High Court, obtaining a stay on the addition of 'McDowell' before the team name and the branding of its team jerseys.

Though Mallya's entry brought money to the clubs and made them more professional, they continued to be dens of politics, what with diverse elements already entrenched in there. This was more so in the case of Mohun Bagan, which had been infiltrated with the men of a leading shipping contractor, Tutu Bose. The entrenched interests wanted to do their own thing. Sometimes this led to legal disputes too.

Mallya had radical ideas: he had Mohun Bagan spawn a new Visa credit card in association with ICICI Bank. Many of these initiatives were not liked by old-time members of the clubs. Moreover, with football being an integral part of the popular culture of Calcutta, the association of the two teams with United Breweries was never even noticed by the public. To that extent the branding of the teams was useless.

In December 2010, Mallya stepped down from the chairmanship of Mohun Bagan after the Asian Football Confederation rules stipulated that a single owner heading two rival football teams would bar the clubs from getting a licence to play in the Asian League. Mallya was more comfortable dealing with East Bengal, so he continued with them, installing his son Siddharth as additional director in the Mohun Bagan company. This arrangement continued for a few years, but as Mallya's troubles grew on the business front, both father and son ultimately quit the football clubs after their own United Spirits was sold off to Diageo.

Disappointed with his experience with the Kolkata football league, Mallya was considering acquisition of a football team in the UK, when the Kingfisher Airlines collapse extinguished all such fancies.

———

Cricket and football are not the only two sports that caught Mallya's interest. His first love was horse racing, and he began backing horses at the races even as a boy. The fact that he lived in Calcutta, which had an active race course, and then in Bangalore, which too had a vibrant racing culture, only made his involvement easy. For some years he had kept away from the races, following his father's advice. But in 1988 he was back in horse racing, not only because of his love for the sport but also because he could see that turf tournaments were good opportunities to brand his lifestyle products like Kingfisher beer. He did not share the prevalent public perception that horse racing was simply another name for gambling. For him it was a sport that required skills and the training of horses and jockeys.

A hindrance to the advancement of horse racing in the country was the lack of good horses resulting from curbs on their import. With liberalization, people's attitude to the pursuit changed, and many stud farms came up in the country. Mallya took over one such farm at Kunigal near Bangalore. This was an over-200-year-old farm set up by Tipu Sultan, the ruler of Mysore, to breed horses for his army. After the fall of Tipu, the farm fell into the hands of the new rulers, and after Independence into the hands of the new state government. It was from the state government of Karnataka that Mallya took over the farm on lease in 1992. He renamed it United Racing & Bloodstock Breeders (URBB).

He would not let off even his animals without somehow associating them with his brands. Before they were readied and dispatched for the derby, they would be branded with the name of Kingfisher at sponsored pre-derby nights. At these events there were glamorous fashion shows featuring top models and film stars. In fact, the Kingfisher Derby was started in 1988 and, in 2010, the McDowell Signature Indian Derby, with prizes upwards of $400,000, became the most lucrative sporting event in India.

Mallya's horses began participating in the Indian derby by 1998 and also won races. But it was clear that he—though interested in horse racing—was more tempted by the branding opportunities this activity presented. To seize these opportunities, he realized he would also require to control the game and the organizations that ran the sport. He proposed many changes, including changes in the telecast of races.

In 2007, he narrowly lost the elections for the position of president at Royal Western India Turf Club. He was very disappointed. He foresaw a decline in his influence. A year later, a further decline in his eminence seemed imminent, when Diageo made an offer of $375,000 for sponsoring the prestigious Indian derby. Later, it upped the offer to $1.1 million. Mallya was ruffled, because for many years now he had been sponsoring the derby. He was not ready to give up his sponsorship of this event; he offered a staggering sum of $4 million to host the event for five years. Naturally, he won the bid.

Motor racing too energized Mallya, and he dreamt of owning a world-class formula racing team, which could (of course) be used to brand his various products. In 2007, he decided Kingfisher would sponsor the Toyota team for the motor racing tournaments. Before the Monaco Grand Prix, he threw a lavish party for the participating team and the organizers of Formula One racing.

The story goes that at the party he found out that one of the teams, Spyker, was in a bad shape financially and proposed to sell out. He immediately began negotiating for it. In a few days' time, he had bought the team in association with Spyker F1 shareholder Michael Moi for a sum of $129 million. From the following season in 2008, the team name was changed to Force India. Shah Rukh Khan was brought in as brand ambassador for the team. With the acquisition of the team, Mallya became even more ambitious: he wanted Formula One racing to come to India and moved the government with a proposal for this.

Before doing this, he got the bosses of F1, which organized Formula One racing, on board. But the Indian government was not at all enthusiastic about the proposal. Implementation of his plans got postponed, from 2009 to 2010 to 2011. However, a racing track was eventually created in Greater Noida, and it was here that the Grand Prix was held between 2012 and 2014. It was not a tremendous success and there were some disputes with the government. In 2011, however, 42 per cent of the ownership of the Force India team was bought over by the Sahara group.

In 2013, the West Indies too started a premier cricket league. In early 2016, Mallya showed interest in acquiring the team Barbados Trident, which was up for grabs. Arriving in Barbados, Mallya told the press: 'I have been coming to the Caribbean since the late 1980s, when I used to own Berger Paints, which had extensive interests in Caribbean. I love this island and obviously that contributed to my enhanced interest in looking at the Tridents franchise.'

Since Mallya was neck-deep in financial trouble, he had to make an indirect bid for the team. He met the prime minister of Barbados privately and pitched for the team. The PM seems to have been floored by him and extended him overwhelming support. He landed the team. As mentioned earlier, he claimed that he had bought the team for only US$100. This claim had few takers. He said there were other shareholders who would pick up the tab and that the Barbados government was also helping with subsidies. The team of Barbados Trident is led by Kieron Pollard. It also has Shoaib Malik and has as its coach Robin Singh.

The Caribbean T-20 league was played between 29 June and 7 August 2016, and although Mallya did not attend the matches (since his passport had been cancelled), he followed the tournament closely sitting in the UK, tweeting on it often. His team, however, fared badly. (Mallya is not the only Indian with a presence in the Caribbean league. Shah Rukh Khan owns the Trinidad & Tobago Red Steel team.)

10

Riding the Real Estate Boom

SOON AFTER DEFEATING TIPU SULTAN in 1799 and occupying the areas controlled by him, the East India Company started looking for a suitable place from where to control the territories of the deposed Mysore nawab. Their first option was to remain in Seringapatam (now Srirangapatna), from where Tipu ran his kingdom, but the English feared its abundance of mosquitoes and wanted an alternative location. Arthur Wellesley, the newly appointed governor of Mysore, who defeated Tipu, proposed Chennapatna and Chitradurga, but in the end Bangalore was chosen.

Wellesley, now busy with other battles, delegated the task of creating the local English government's new headquarters to a rather junior military engineer, John Blakistone. Barely twenty-four in 1809, Blakistone was asked to figure out where exactly in Bangalore a new British cantonment could be established. The industrious Blakistone, after surveying dozens of locations in Bangalore, fixed the capital in a specific area that he described as 'by far the pleasantest and most agreeable residence in the peninsula because of its geographical location and favourable climate'.

Twenty villages west of Ulsoor lake were taken over, and thus Bangalore Cantonment came to be established. The cantonment housed not only the military but also other English establishments. This development had far-reaching effects, influencing what would happen here more than a century later. After the administration of Bangalore reverted to the Wodeyar kings of Mysore in 1885 and the cantonment became a civil and military station, this area became the most sought after place in the city for the elite. The trend continued even after Independence, and this zone still remains a kind of exclusive enclave.

Established in these parts in 1885 was also the factory of Bangalore Breweries, an outfit that used to supply beer to British soldiers, not only in Bangalore but everywhere in the peninsula up to Poona. The brewery was located on a 22-acre plot on Grant Road, barely a kilometre and a half from the best-known part of the civil and military area, the South Parade. After Independence, this road was renamed Mahatma Gandhi Road, now popularly known as M.G. Road.

After taking over United Breweries (of which Bangalore Breweries was a part), Vittal Mallya decided to make the premises of the factory his official headquarters. A spacious bungalow set on a 6-acre plot served as his residence. The British parts of Bangalore went by British-sounding names, the neighbourhood in which the UB factory stood being called MacIver Town (after L.J. MacIver, who was collector and president of the Municipal Commission of the Civil and Military Station in 1934-35). The neighbourhood sat on the edge of Cubbon Park, the lung of Bangalore, which made it a very pleasant place.

Until the early 1990s, prime properties in Bangalore

and elsewhere in the country had no great value other than their being thought of as excellent neighbourhoods. But the economic liberalization of 1991 unleashed frenzied activity in the real estate sector. Many individuals and corporations that owned land and other real estate began unlocking it, milking it for its full value.

Vijay Mallya loved the good life, loved opulence and loved grandeur. The 6-acre compound, where many of his cars could be parked to show them off, was something he cherished. He would not part with such a property for its commercial value. He settled in deeper, proposing in the early 1990s to the municipal corporation of Bangalore that Grant Road, on which his home and UB's factory stood, be renamed Vittal Mallya Road. Considering that nobody knew who Grant was, this was not a difficult proposition. But the Bangalore Mahanagara Palike had its conditions: UB must take up responsibility for the upkeep of Grant Road, though the municipality would continue to be in charge of garbage clearance. For Mallya this had a larger implication: renaming the road after his father meant he was turning the entire neighbourhood into his very own personal zone.

Bangalore began to dazzle in the late '90s as it rapidly emerged as the Silicon Valley of India. Until now it had been just a laid-back colonial town. The city was now the destination of technology companies from all over the world. It became increasingly cosmopolitan as people from around the country moved in. As the demand for housing and commercial space grew, realty prices and rentals also surged. Overnight, those who had no other asset but a house they had bought dirt cheap years ago found themselves wealthy. Skyscrapers rose in the city and there was demand for more.

Mallya now saw a great opportunity staring him in the face. He had not wanted to part with his magnificent estate, but he was too practical to let go of such a mammoth opportunity. It did not make sense to have a factory on a 10-acre plot of land in a prime area of Bangalore and live there on 6 acres. Five acres owned by him had already been donated a long time ago to the Jesuit Society, which had built St Joseph's Indian High School on it. Mallya began to consider how he could now turn his prime estate into a cash cow. With the beer factory that stood on the site not large enough to take care of demand, a bigger factory had been established at Nelamangala on the outskirts of the city.

Thus was conceived UB City. Work on UB City—billed to be the biggest commercial property in Bangalore—began in 2004. It was a joint venture of Vijay Mallya, United Breweries and the Prestige group, which had many real estate projects going in the city. Planned on 13 acres of land, UB City would carry 93,000 square metres of high-end commercial, retail and service apartment space. It would have four towers: UB Towers (nineteen floors), Comet (eleven floors), Canberra (seventeen floors) and Concorde (nineteen floors). The project was completed four years later.

UB Towers, into which all the UB Group offices shifted, stood 123 metres high, making it the tallest building in Bangalore and Karnataka. Concorde is 115 metres tall, and Canberra 105 metres. The first three levels of Concorde and Canberra are the retail area, constituting a luxury mall named 'The Collection'. Top international brands, including Rolex, Burberry, Louis Vuitton and Canali, have their stores here. High-end restaurants serve a range of world and Indian cuisines. The mall has fine-dining options as well as cafes. Of course, there are pubs and hangout places too for those craving the night life. The complex also contains service apartments, branded Oakwood, a five-star hotel (J.W. Marriott) and a 1,000-seat amphitheatre for plays and music shows. A three-level parking facility accommodates 1,600 cars. UB City is truly a one-stop business and lifestyle hub. All the top Indian corporations, from the Tatas to the Birlas to Reliance, have their offices in UB City. Commercial rentals are the highest here in the city. For this reason, a lot of its space is still unoccupied.

There was much speculation that Mallya would construct a residential complex too in UB City. But he had denied any plans of the sort. However, in September 2009, while briefing shareholders of UB (Holdings) Ltd—the parent company of the UB Group—Mallya let slip: 'We have got permission to develop an additional 500,000 square feet of space in UB City. This has come about due to changes in the zonal regulations of the area, which has resulted in an increase in the floor area ratio.' On the sidelines, Mallya managers told journalists that a residential complex was being planned.

A year later, in 2010, while announcing the fourth quarter results of UB (Holdings), Mallya also announced that 'a joint development agreement with a developer had been signed on 26 April 2010 for the development of a luxury residential building in the available land in UB City.'

Of course, this meant his existing residence would have to be razed. The luxury residential complex would be named Kingfisher Towers. Its high-end flats, each 8,200 square feet, would be sold at Rs 20 crore a-piece. This price was later revised to Rs 30 crore. A penthouse perched right on top of the building was to be built for Mallya himself. This would be his pie in the sky. Three blocks containing eighty-two apartments, on a developable area of 1.09 million square feet, would be constructed. Only seventy-two were to be sold; ten would be distributed among the Mallya family members. An earlier plan for 100 flats of different sizes was discarded as it could potentially lead to ego problems between the elite flat owners!

The apartment complex would have five entrances, one exclusively for Mallya. His penthouse would resemble White House—his original home. Only, instead of standing on earth it would be up in the sky. The two-storeyed penthouse, on levels 33 and 34, would cover 40,000 square feet. It would contain a wine cellar, a heated indoor pool, an outdoor infinity pool, a gym, a salon and a spa, among other facilities. It would provide views of not only Cubbon Park but also of the Vidhana Soudha and all the major landmarks in the city. To cap it all, the penthouse would have a helipad on its roof.

The ordinary flat owners would have access to a common garden area of 25,000 square feet at the ground level, a 6,000-square-foot club house on the fifth floor, a swimming pool on the tenth, a badminton court, a party hall and a terrace garden.

But, as Mallya's debts mounted, the Karnataka High Court, on 18 August 2014, restrained UB Holdings from selling its flats in Kingfisher Towers. Many had already been sold, but many were still unsold.

While the quiet area of Vittal Mallya Road—Shanthala Nagar—has transformed into a swanky, high-fashion street with swish pubs, a Lamborghini showroom and expensive restaurants, old-time residents of the area have been bristling. They are often quoted in the local papers, complaining of poor civic services, lamenting that nobody takes care of the roads despite the upkeep agreement between the UB group and the municipality. They have to contend with broken tiles and potholes on the roads by day, and with drunken roadside brawls by night. Electricity cables hang dangerously low. Some locals also complain that only half of Vittal Mallya Road—the portion just outside UB City—is cleaned and maintained by the UB group, and the rest is left unkempt.

Residents of the area later got together to create a welfare association and an improvement group to take up the responsibility for the mess themselves. There was also a controversy about UB City promoters having violated building rules, and the matter was referred to the Lokayukta of Karnataka. Another allegation was that UB City had encroached on Vittal Mallya Road and the municipal authorities had looked the other way. The building had eaten into the footpath too and closed a part of the storm water drain.

The complaints snowballed, and ultimately it was a threat from the municipality to revert to the old name of Grant Road that made Mallya sit up. He realized that the run-down road stood in ugly contrast to the top brands sitting in his mall. The road quality should live up to the name of UB City, he decided. Now he partnered with the Prestige group to refurbish the road at a cost of Rs 6 crore, 55 per cent of it to be borne by UB and the remaining 45 per cent by Prestige. The project was overseen by the municipal authorities, and in June 2010 a brand new street with granite slab-covered pavements was opened by the chief minister of Karnataka. A bust of Vittal Mallya was unveiled on the occasion.

UB City has been an extremely controversial project.

The pricing of its super luxury flats was one contentious point. Even though real estate prices are not regulated by the government, there is an official reference rate for real estate in Bangalore and in all other cities in India. This is determined by the local authorities for the purpose of calculating property tax. However, in reality, most real estate deals involve a cash component, so the government figures are always an underestimate of the real price. Since Mallya believed in the dictum of 'the higher the price of a good, the better its quality', he initially priced his flats at Rs 33,000 per square foot. But this was colossally ambitious, and no buyer was willing to pay that kind of money over the table. In 2011, the civic authorities in Bangalore 'fixed' the selling price of Mallya's flats at Rs 11,000 per square foot. But the government revised this price two years later, in August 2013, to around Rs 16,750 per square foot.

As Mallya's troubles mounted on the Kingfisher Airlines front, he began contemplating the sale of at least a part of UB City. The *Times of India*, Bangalore, reported on 1 May 2012 that UB Holdings was in talks with private equity firms Blackstone and Kohlberg Kravis Roberts (KKR) to 'unlock the value of its office spaces' including the iconic UB Towers. As part of the agreement, the property would be leased back to Mallya immediately after the sale. And there was also an indication that after the end of a specified period, the property would be sold to Mallya as part of a buyback arrangement.

A few months later, on 26 February 2013, the *Mint* reported that the deal under discussion with the PE firms had fallen through. The parties to the deal had disagreements on the valuation of the property. Apparently, Mallya wanted more than what the firms were ready to pay—he was said to be valuing the property at Rs 850 crore. From time to time, however, speculation about Mallya selling UB City still appears in the press, keeping the kettle boiling.

In early 2017, advertisements aggressively marketing the luxury four-bedroom flats in Kingfisher Towers began appearing on some websites. At Rs 35,000 a square foot, the price of each flat was Rs 29.12 crore. Buyers were offered almost immediate possession but, at that price, the response was poor.

11

The King of Good Times

AN INDIVIDUAL'S PERSONALITY DEVELOPS quite early in life, and by the time he grows up, the traits peculiar to him are quite set. Also, his personality is partly shaped by genetic factors and partly by his early life experiences.

Vijay Mallya is known as the 'king of good times' and has been covered extensively in the media for his opulent ways. But very little light has been shed on how he acquired his taste for this life—a life that revolved around multiple residences across continents, yacht parties, fashionable friends and young beauties. His larger-than-life personality and his overwhelming desire to project it have never been analysed.

Vijay is a person very different from his father. Vittal Mallya was a very successful entrepreneur who built his fortune from scratch. He was also a man who counted his pennies and made note of all his expenses, always trying to limit them to the severe minimum. It is not this side of Vittal's personality that influenced Vijay, at least early on. Vittal and his first wife, Lalitha Ramaiah (Vijay's mother), separated when Vijay was not quite eleven. Vittal remained in Bangalore, while Vijay and Lalitha went back to Calcutta.

The choice of Calcutta was natural: the family had lived here before migrating to Bangalore. Although the two were well provided for, their life did not reflect any opulence. Their life was like that of any other upper middle class family.

However, Vijay would have seen that his father's new family was better off, with the fortunes of the liquor empire being on the constant upswing. That Vittal never made it explicit to Vijay that he would inherit his empire may have also contributed to the young boy's sense of insecurity. In fact, Vittal often dropped hints that Vijay could only have his empire if he proved to be good in his studies. The fear that his father could disinherit him is likely to have dogged Vijay in his growing-up years. But Vijay was not an open rebel: in all probability this was because Vittal was not unkind to Vijay or to his mother Lalitha. The overconfidence he projected in his adult life, though, could be traced back to his childhood insecurities.

Mallya himself spoke about his growing-up days to talk show host Simi Garewal in her interview series *Rendezvous* some time in the late 1990s. He recounted how he longed to meet his father, whom he did not get to have 'enough of'. He said he felt lonely as an only child with no siblings and used to be bothered about how he was not part of his father's life in Bangalore where he stayed with his new family. He recalled his happy childhood in Bangalore before his parents separated, mixing with the children who stayed on the UB campus.

One of his friends at that time was Kiran Mazumdar, the well-known biotech entrepreneur of today. 'We lived a charmed life in the residential community of United Breweries,' she says. She, her brother, Vijay and his two cousins called themselves the 'famous five' (after the adventure heroes of children's writer Enid Blyton's series). They would race bikes, play cricket, drive in Vijay's toy Ferrari and even bully him.

In the same interview to Garewal, Mallya recounted how his father maintained a diary of daily expenses, including the smallest amount spent. Once he lost a one-paisa coin and his father noted it down: 'Re 0.01 lost by Vijay'. As he grew up, he reacted in his own way to his father's niggardly tendencies. He became a spendthrift. Ultimately, this came to define his personality. He did not hesitate to spend lavishly on his offices. His father may have been bothered but did not stop him, publicly at least.

However, this sense of alienation from his father did not result in any anger against him. After all, his father was responsible for grooming him for a business career. He recollected that his father did not take him under his wing but at the same time ensured that his work was effectively supervised. The father ensured that proper work values were inculcated in the son.

In school and college, Vijay dealt with his pangs of loneliness by making a lot of friends who embraced him as part of their family. Even today, wherever he goes, he is always surrounded by a large entourage of friends.

Influences from one's school too play a major role in shaping one's character. Vijay's primary schooling was at Sophia High School in Bangalore. In Calcutta, he went to La Martiniere for boys, a school started in 1836. It was located not far from Minto Park where Vijay stayed. It was originally run by the British for the benefit of their boys but went on to admit elite Indians. 'The influences of La Martiniere can be seen in him. He is like a pucca sahib, and the fact that he loves England and London is the result of his education at La Martinere,' says one of Mallya's contemporaries at school. 'Our school laid great stress on learning English, and Vijay's command over English is extraordinarily good. This is the result of his schooling.'

He also attributes Mallya's good grooming to the school. He was a member of Hastings House, named after British-era Governor General Warren Hastings, while in Class XI, and was also the house captain. The colour for the house was red, the reason, some say, behind his liking for the colour. His love of music is also attributed to his education: the school stressed a lot on this. His mother Lalitha, quoted in a volume brought out on his fiftieth birthday, has talked about her son's interest in sports, dramatics and NCC in school. She also revealed that in his final year in school, he was recommended for the school's good conduct award, missing it narrowly to a friend who insisted that both of them be given the award jointly. But not all of his contemporaries in school have good things to say about him.

'He was a spoilt child and everybody knew he had a lot of money that he was willing to throw,' says the editor of *Economic and Political Weekly*, Paranjoy Guha Thakurta, who was Mallya's senior by one year in school. But Paranjoy also remembers how, when a cricket game had to be played and there were no kits available, Vijay immediately bought an entire kit for the team.

Vijay was also a very friendly person, right from childhood, his mother remembers. Once, at the end of a holiday in Jaipur, when he was eight, the hosts told Lalitha to leave him behind as he had become very friendly with their children. He was indulged now and then, but never spoilt, says his mother.

———

The liquor baron is also a very religious man, though he does not appear to be so. Born into a Brahmin family, he grew up seeing his mother and grandmother at their rituals, and some of this rubbed off on him too. He is a great devotee of Lord Balaji at Tirumala, and loses no opportunity to worship there. He makes large donations to the temple. The attendants there who accompany visitors from the guest house to the temple talk about how lavish he was in tipping them. Each Kingfisher plane, upon induction into the company's fleet, would be flown to Tirupati to circle the temple in the air to obtain Lord Balaji's blessings. But his darshan at Tirupati was not that of a common pilgrim's. The *Times of India*'s Hyderabad edition once reported that the temple trust chairman D.K. Audikesavulu, who was Mallya's liquor bottler, would escort him in for darshan that could extend for one-and-a-half hours while the regular pilgrims' entry would be halted for some time, leading to long queues at the temple.

Mallya also does the Sabarimala yatra, observing the forty-day period of abstinence that precedes it. During this time he can be seen dressed in black, following the tradition of Sabarimala devotees. Of course, his black clothes are well designed. After this preparation, he treks the 6 km pathway to the temple, taking the steps all the way up. Since his turning thirty, he had hardly missed this annual pilgrimage. Every day Mallya does puja on his laptop, even when he is flying.

The temple-going habit was inculcated in him from a young age: at five he was accompanying his grandparents on their temple visits. His grandfather would tell him stories from the Mahabharata and the Ramayana, and his familiarity with mantras and slokas came from hearing his grandmother recite them. He also wears pendants bearing images of Lord Shiva, Lord Balaji and the Lord of Sringeri.

Apart from being a deeply religious man, he is also moderately conservative. He goes a lot by the stars, never negotiating any deals during rahu kalam, that inauspicious one-and-a-half-hour period which falls at a different but specific time each day of the week. He is also influenced by some of the modern-day godmen, one of them being Art of Living founder Sri Sri Ravi Shankar.

Mallya wanted to become a doctor, like his grandfather, but ended up doing a bachelor's degree in commerce from St Xavier's College in Calcutta, joining his father's business afterwards. St Xavier's too is a very old institution, dating back to 1860. Vijay's name is prominently displayed on the college website as an alumnus of the institution. Though he did not become a medical doctor, fifteen-odd years into his working life, he was able to get an honorary doctorate in business management from the University of South California in Irving in 1997. Ever since obtaining the title, he prefer to be addressed as Dr Vijay Mallya.

Whatever respect he later commanded, at the time Mallya joined the liquor industry, the lay public looked down on people in that business. His quest to diversify into many other businesses may have been an attempt to gain respectability in society. His expensive tastes and lavish ways could also be a manifestation of the same desire. Perhaps, even without realizing it, his quest for respectability superseded his sense of proportion, leading to the excesses he is infamous for today. In his mind he was justifying all his actions, arguing that they were for the sake of his business.

He dropped a hint of this in an interview he gave to theatre personality Lillete Dubey on a lifestyle TV channel. The details of the interview were reproduced in *DNA* on 21 April 2006. Dubey asked Mallya whether his wife minded his being seen in the news with many gorgeous women. He answered: 'She understands my business and my personality. She lets me do what I need to do. I am the brand ambassador for my brands. They are associated with high life.'

His Kingfisher calendar brought him in close proximity to glamorous models. The calendar was intended to promote the Kingfisher brand. Its pictures of attractive models in bikinis were shot at a different exotic locale every year by top fashion photographer Atul Kasbekar. The calendar, which was first published in 2003, launched some top Bollywood heroines, such as Deepika Padukone, Katrina Kaif and Nargis Fakhri, and some lesser-known actors such as Esha Gupta, Yana Gupta, Poonam Pandey and Bruna Abdulla. Often, the locales were chosen by Mallya himself. The calendar has been shot in Mauritius, the French Riviera, the Andaman Islands, and in many other places. In 2010 the calendar went a step further, introducing the Kingfisher Calendar Model Hunt to select the supermodels who would feature in the exclusive calendar. The annual competition is televised by NDTV Good Times and is a much-followed programme.

Like his father, Mallya is a much-married man. He met his first wife while flying Air India in the early 1980s. In those days Air India flew only internationally, and great care was taken by the management in the hiring of air hostesses. Mallya used to fly only Air India as a result of a diktat from his father that UB staffers only travel by the national carrier. He took a fancy to Samira Tyabji, who came from a well-known Mumbai family, and soon the two were seeing each other. They got married, and their son Siddharth was born in 1987.

The marriage did not last long. In 1993, Mallya married Rekha, a long-time neighbour from Bangalore. Rekha had been married twice before (once to Coorg coffee planter Pratap Chettiappa and then to businessman Shahid Mehmood) and had three children. But Vijay looked after them as if they were his own. In fact, he formally adopted one of the daughters, Laila, marrying her off in style in Bali years later. Mallya and Rekha continue to be married, though she stays abroad, away from her husband. Rekha is a low-key person, always preferring to stay in the background.

Since 2011, Mallya has been seen with another woman, Pinky Lalwani. On 2 March 2016, when he left India, Lalwani was with him. With him sinking deeper into trouble, she has, to all appearances, gotten closer to him. *Mumbai Mirror* reported on 27 May 2013 that at the annual billionaires' party on the occasion of the Monaco Grand Prix weekend held on Mallya's superyacht *Indian Empress*, Lalwani was introduced as his girlfriend. There were 600 guests at the party, including Monaco's Prince Albert and his wife. Lalwani had once been an air hostess with Kingfisher Airlines.

'As early as 2006 we knew that Vijay was going around with Pinky. There were many stories about Pinky and how

Vijay's car would go to fetch her. Once I saw her in the cabin of a Kingfisher flight, and by mistake I blurted out: "Oh you are Pinky!",' says a former senior executive with UB.

In the interview with Dubey, Mallya was asked his views on fidelity. He replied that fidelity was not necessarily linked to marriage; it was something that invoked an element of trust. If you cannot stick to your commitment, you state so and get out of it, he said, adding that infidelity appeared to imply doing things behind somebody's back. 'That's not something I do,' he said. Dubey pressed on, asking whether this meant that he was in favour of 'khullam khulla pyar'. He answered: 'My life is an open book. Those who love me appreciate it and take me for what I am.'

———

Everything that Mallya does is in excess. He owns many luxury homes across the world though some of them have been sold after his financial troubles began. Clifton Estate, on Nettleton Road in Cape Town in South Africa, has one of the most expensive properties in the country. Mallya's property, bought in 2010, is in this locality. Rumoured to have been sold recently, this property has a sweeping view of Clifton beach, counted as among the best beaches in the world. The super-luxury house on the property has a sauna, a gym and garage space for four cars. He has in the past hosted movie stars, singers and royalty there. He has thrown lavish parties on its patio, which flanks a 25-metre-long infinity pool. This place is believed to have been sold now.

Mallya's property in the thirty-nine-storey Trump Plaza

on 61st Street in New York is a penthouse. The residential building is one of the costliest properties in the city and overlooks the New York bay. US President Donald Trump has his home here. Mallya brought this property too in 2010. It is not certain if he sold it in 2014.

On the other side of the US, he has a house in Sausalito in the San Francisco Bay area in California. Sausalito, close to the north end of the Golden Gate bridge, has a landscape that is both hill-top and beach. His 11,000-square-foot house, bought in 1987, is one of the most prominent in the town. It has a view stretching from Belvedere to Bay Bridge and San Francisco. According to a report in *Mint* on 10 March 2016, Mallya was in California with his pregnant wife Samira when she fell ill. She was advised to rest for a few months and not travel. He bought this home so she could stay there.

In the UK, he owns multiple properties—a house on Baker Street in London, a country house in Tewin village in Hertfordshire and a castle in Scotland. Keillam Castle is located in Perthshire. Built in 1877 at the site of an older, thirteenth-century castle that got burnt down, the estate is known for its magnificent woodland garden created under a canopy of trees.

According to the same *Mint* report, the 25,000-acre Mabula Game Reserve on the outskirts of Johannesburg is also owned by Mallya. His other properties include Le Grande Jardin, which is on Sainte Marguerite, the largest of the Lerins Islands on the French Riviera. Mallya bought this property in 2008, against stiff competition from celebrities and billionaires from Russia. Many of his high-profile parties have been on this island.

Of course, Mallya owns many properties in India. Apart from the White House that he is building at the top of Kingfisher Towers in Bangalore, he owns a house called Devika in the tony locality of Sardar Patel Marg in New Delhi. He used to live here as a Rajya Sabha MP. In Mumbai he owns a sea-facing bungalow, Niladri, on the posh Napean Sea Road. This has been the venue for all his Kingfisher calendar launch parties.

The most well-known of his mansions is his Goa property. Kingfisher Villa, on Sinquerim beach in Candolim village, is palatial and decorated in the typical Goan style with handcrafted teak furniture. The property has ponds, swimming pools and a massive dance floor that doubles up as a helipad. *India Today*, in its 16 May 2016 issue, reported that a fleet of luxury cars, including a red Ferrari, was usually parked inside the property. The property has now been taken over by the SBI after Mallya reneged on his agreement to repay loans taken from it. It was sold in April 2017 and picked up by businessman Sachin Joshi for Rs 73 crore. Mallya also owns – through Mandwa Farms Private Limited – a 17-acre beach-facing farmhouse worth Rs 100 crore in Alibagh. The ED took possession of the farmhouse in the middle of May 2017.

Mallya also owns 260 vintage cars, bicycles and race cars, all housed in a special private museum he owns in California. He has a special collection manager who acquires these vehicles. The collection can only be seen by private invitation.

The oldest car in the collection is a 1913-vintage Rolls-Royce Silver Ghost. The other distinctive machines in the collection are a 1955 Porsche 55 Rs Spyden (racing car), a

1955 Mercedes-Benz SLR 300, a 1954 Jaguar D Type (racing car), a 1957 Ford Thunderbird, a Ford Model A and a 1972 Ferrari Dino Spider.

———

Mallya's every action reflects opulence or excess. When he visited the studio where Garewal interviewed him, a huge stretch van followed him. It was stocked with hundreds of shirts, suits and ties, neatly arranged. Mallya showed them to her and asked her to choose what she would like him to wear on her show.

He also makes frequent style changes to his appearance. 'Sometimes he has long hair, sometimes short. Sometimes he sports a beard and other times he takes it off. He has hundreds of appearances,' says a United Breweries manager, unwilling to be identified. 'He is also very fond of diamonds—in his ear, on rings and on bracelets.'

Most of Mallya's staffers loved working with him. 'He is a very quick decision maker and this is not because he reacts quickly but because he understands fast,' says the manager. As for his women staffers, he is a super-hero to them; many of them describe him in gushing tones. 'Oh, he is no nice. So considerate. We are proud to work in his company. Some mistakes he may have made, but he is very energetic. I love him,' says a former manager who was in her mid-thirties when in Mallya's employ.

While in Bangalore, Mallya used to operate mostly from his home. 'He would give us an appointment at his home. But the waiting period before you got to see him was very long. You could order for lunch, tea, snacks from his home kitchen while you waited. So we did not mind waiting for him. The actual meeting was only for a few minutes because he would clear the matter that we took to him quickly,' the manager says. Other staffers point out that although Mallya indeed partied hard, he also worked very hard.

Mallya had a reputation for arriving late for meetings, and often kept important visitors waiting very long. 'Sometimes, if there was a meeting in Mumbai at, say, 6.30 p.m., he would leave Bangalore in his private jet at 6 p.m. You can imagine how late he would be,' says a senior executive at UB. Nobody is sure why he made people wait so long. 'The best answer is that he was not so good at time management,' a manager says.

Ravi Nedungadi, UB's finance chief for many years, described in an interview how Mallya would dominate any space he entered. Once he decided to go for a walk in Mumbai's Nariman Point, from his own office to the office of a financial institution a few hundred yards away. He was dressed in black as he was preparing for the annual Sabarimala pilgrimage, and had grown a luxuriant beard and long hair. Leading the way was a staffer wielding an umbrella like a music conductor, and behind him two gun-toting security men. They were followed by Mallya, who had two burly South African bodyguards on either side. The rear was made up by two senior executives. Activity on the busy sidewalks came to a halt, with everyone staring at the procession, Nedungadi said.

Tushita Patel, a journalist and Mallya's one-time political secretary, said in an interview that he was a prime example of the kind of man who never stops working and has no conventional working hours. She was offered her job at 1.30

a.m. on the phone, she said. His day never ended with any correspondence left on the table. 'Defying science, body clock and time zones, he is perpetually in the throes of meetings. Three secretaries change shifts, but VJM keeps working,' she wrote in the volume brought out on Mallya's fiftieth anniversary. Writing in a similar vein, Vijay Rekhi, a top executive at UB, described how Mallya packed thirty-six hours into twenty-four. Sometimes he began his meetings after midnight, as energetic as he was by day, although the staff would be straining hard to keep their attention focused. Some staffers remember him as a man with a memory of amazing accuracy for conversations, numbers, people and places. He was apparently fluent in many languages—English, Kannada, Bengali and French, and a great mimic and storyteller. 'Sometimes at parties he perfectly mimics one of his senior managers and regales all the rest,' says a Mallya manager.

Those who know him say Mallya is very particular that his image project 'exclusivity'. He was never comfortable with the masses. This was true even when he dealt with the press. He was chary of holding press conferences (not that he never did) but knew some journalists personally and would directly communicate with them on the phone. Like many other corporate captains, he would not meet every journalist who sought an appointment with him, even if they were from leading publications. Journalists who have dealt with him say he meets newspersons when he needs them.

'I was about to do a story on Kingfisher when they first reneged on their payments to oil companies for supply of aviation turbine fuel for their planes. Mallya's public relations manager organized my meeting with him. He was very conciliatory, and told me in Kannada not to screw his happiness by writing such a story. He pleaded that I should try and understand his predicament,' says journalist B.V. Shivashankar. The story was done, but the next time the journalist wrote about the UB group, Mallya got his PR team to prevail upon the management of the newspaper group to kill the story.

Old-timers in Bangalore also remember how a correspondent of a leading newspaper had to tender a personal apology on the pages of his newspaper when a story of his offended Mallya, who took up the matter with the proprietor. Incidentally, the journalist was the same one who had—in a late-night news-break—reported Mallya's arrest in 1987 at the airport. The correspondent was working for another paper at that time, and was the only journalist who had put out the story.

In 1986, when Mallya was in the midst of an aborted effort to take over Shaw Wallace, journalist Paranjoy Guha Thakurta tried to visit him at his office. 'He made me sit outside his office for two hours but never saw me. But three years ago he suddenly called me and asked whether I could share a report on paid news that I had written for the Press Council of India. This is Mallya for you. If he needs you he will jump for you otherwise he won't recognize you,' says Paranjoy.

Mallya's public relations department decided to bring out a special book to mark his fiftieth birthday. The book would contain what fifty of his close associates in life—from his mother to business associates to even his corporate rivals— had to say about him. All fifty were told to keep the plan secret from Mallya. But at the last stage, when printing of the book was about to commence, he learnt about the plan and hit the roof. He immediately demanded that the contents of the book be shown to him, in particular because he learnt that long-time rivals had also been asked to comment about him. He is said to have gone through every page carefully and cleared the contents. He also asked for inclusion of comments from two other people. But he was very happy when he received the final copy of the book.

Mallya was also very particular about his personal stationery and the gifts that would go out in his name. 'He personally finalized the gifts and approved them. Also, he has class, he would never hold a meeting in any place other than at a top five-star hotel,' points out a UB manager. He said Mallya would also insist that all his senior managers on tour stayed in top hotels. 'He believed that a manager represents his brand and if he stayed at a middling hotel that would reflect badly on his company,' the UB manager said. Not surprisingly, all his top managers were remunerated and looked after very well, and Mallya was on very friendly terms with them, exchanging jokes and anecdotes with them through text and WhatsApp messages. 'Mallya lived beyond his means and allowed his staff to enjoy. There was no cost consciousness. Everybody was a maharaja and that's why all his staff swear by him,' says Bangalore-based chartered accountant C. Shankar.

Dilip Maitra, a business journalist in Bangalore who tracked Mallya closely for many years, feels Mallya is deliberately late to meetings and calculatedly makes people wait. 'He is like a zamindar with a large ego, to whom nobody can say no,' says Maitra. The journalist says that Mallya was present at his headquarters in Bangalore only once in a while, so when he was there all his top managers would start queueing up from the morning, hoping to meet him. He would, however, make his appearance only at noontime or later, and dismiss the managers one by one after dealing with them in a summary fashion. Maitra says he was witness to the conglomeration of managers at Mallya's home because he too had been given time for an interview there.

'The scene was reminiscent of the house of a zamindar, where peasants and other favour-seekers would be waiting and the zamindar would show up after hours and dispose of them in minutes. When he was happy his generosity was unbounded, but God forbid if he got angry,' says Maitra. Other journalists who have interacted with Mallya are also of the opinion that he is a 'big show-off', acting like a feudal chief in flaunting his wealth and connections.

Maitra does not think Mallya has any great business sense either: 'Like many others obsessed with their ego, he can be fooled by those seeking to fool him. A good example is how the Chhabria brothers took him for a ride for two decades before he got hold of Shaw Wallace. I have heard him fulminate so many times about the Chhabria brothers in frustration.'

'You cannot say he is a bad businessman. He got into a crisis because he is a great gambler. Sooner or later he had to get into trouble,' says V. Subramanian, who worked with Mallya for twelve years, the last five as his executive assistant. He recollects the day when Mallya inducted him as his executive assistant from his earlier role in the corporate planning department. 'He asked me whether I wanted to operate out of Dubai or Bangalore, and I asked him what my job description would be. Mallya told me, "You can do anything, you can go anywhere. But whatever you do, wherever you go should be in the interest of the company".'

Being an executive assistant to Mallya was like being an officer on special duty, says Subramanian. 'He gave a lot of independence to his managers and was fully trusting. He was a regal man and all of us were impressed by him. The attrition rates were very low in the UB group.' He remembers how all his colleagues would get extremely nervous on the day of the annual general meeting, as that was the only day that the chairman would be exposed to all sorts of questioning by the shareholders. But Mallya would come out unscathed from the AGM, even if he appeared unprepared.

Eminent journalist and now Union minister M.J. Akbar wrote in the commemorative volume about Mallya in 2005 that 'the fundamental facet of his personality is that he is a romantic. He has the romance of an adventurer.' Akbar felt that if Mallya had to be compared with a Mughal emperor it would be with Babur and not someone like Shah Jahan, because at heart Mallya is an entrepreneur. 'He is the kind of man who can give finance chiefs ulcers. I have seen Vijay fail but not defeated,' Akbar wrote.

The million-dollar question is whether Mallya will be able to withstand the knock delivered by Kingfisher.

12

The Bankers' Bane

IN SEPTEMBER 2009, VIJAY MALLYA had a meeting with Yogesh Agarwal, chairman of IDBI Bank. Kingfisher Airlines was sinking, but Mallya had lobbied with the top guns at North Block to get a loan sanctioned for the company. Agarwal had been appointed as the chairman at IDBI Bank (earlier Industrial Development Bank of India) to oversee the conversion of this development banking institution into a full-service commercial bank. As a development bank, it could not take deposits, with the result that it had little money to lend. This had severely restricted its operations, leaving it with no resources to develop industrial projects.

Mallya's sources had told him that if any banker was willing to lend money to Kingfisher Airlines, it would be Agarwal, who was reputed to be aggressively resourceful. An engineer from BITS, Pilani, Agarwal wanted to be seen as somebody who was truly promoting economic growth. Mallya made the right noises with the banker: his airline was suffering because of its stepmotherly treatment by the government. The airline sector was capital-intensive, and government imposts and taxes made it doubly difficult for any entrepreneur to make a success of an airline venture. He also complained that the industry was not operating on a level playing field. The government had pumped in thousands of crores of rupees to run Air India, which was going from bad to worse, but would not spare a single penny for private airlines such as his. Only a forward-looking banker like Agarwal could understand his predicament.

Agarwal sympathized with Mallya but realized that it would not be perfectly in order to lend money to Kingfisher. With its negative net worth and its eroded capital base, it did not fulfil IDBI Bank's criteria for lending. But he was under great pressure from North Block. The question before Agarwal was whether he could overlook Kingfisher's declared losses of Rs 1,600 crore in March 2009. But Mallya, being an MP and a VIP, could not be taken lightly. Resisting the top mandarins in North Block would not augur well for Agarwal in the future. He was looking forward to a plum posting after his retirement, and remaining on good terms with the government, which had just got re-elected for a second five-year term, would help. Agarwal was like a once-bitten-twice-shy kid. A probationary officer of the 1972 batch at the SBI, he had lost the chairmanship of the bank to his batchmate, O.P. Bhatt. Following stiff competition with Agarwal, first for the post of managing director of SBI, Bhatt had gone on to become the chairman of the largest lender in the country. Agarwal did become MD of SBI but was soon obliged to leave the post and head to IDBI.

A few days after Mallya called on Agarwal, A. Raghunathan, the CFO of Kingfisher Airlines, put up a proposal for a corporate loan of Rs 950 crore on 1 October 2009, marking it to B.K. Batra, executive director at the bank. On 6 October, even before this proposal could be processed, he requested the bank to lend Rs 150 crore for a period of six months, referring to the meeting between Mallya and Agarwal. This money was required to pay Kingfisher's overseas vendors. This proposal was taken post haste to the credit committee of the bank by Batra and approved on 7 October, a day after it was submitted. The committee consisted of Batra himself and three other senior officials of the bank, O.V. Bundellu, R. Bansal and S.K.V. Srinivasan.

Almost at the same time, Raghunathan wrote another letter to Batra seeking ad hoc release of Rs 200 crore. Batra, who was in charge of corporate banking, forwarded the letter to Agarwal, recommending approval of the request. It was obvious that IDBI Bank was finding it difficult to clear a huge loan of Rs 950 crore to a loss-making company, and that Kingfisher Airlines was working around its resistance by breaking up its loan requirement into smaller amounts. Its initial application for Rs 950 crore continued to be alive. Little wonder then that the request for Rs 200 crore too was cleared by Agarwal, the amount subsumed into the total loan of Rs 950 crore applied for. Soon after the loan was approved on 4 November, the amounts sanctioned were disbursed.

The original proposal of Rs 950 crore was finally brought to the bank's credit committee on 19 November 2009. Predictably, it was cleared, and Rs 750 crore was released to Kingfisher on 27 November. In approving the loan, the bank did not heed the observations of the airline's auditors, who had noted that funds amounting to Rs 4,630 crore raised earlier by the airline on a short-term basis were used for long-term purposes. Moreover, an undisputed TDS amount of more than Rs 100 crore had not been deposited for over six months. To cap this, the airline's credit rating was not available.

However, in an attempt to cover its exposure to Kingfisher, IDBI Bank accepted as security the hypothecation and assignment of the Kingfisher brand. It was argued in the internal note put up to the bank's credit committee that the Kingfisher brand was very valuable; Mallya had made much of his fortunes by hawking his beer under that brand name. Interestingly, by accepting its brand name as collateral, Kingfisher could be given loans at a lower rate of interest. IDBI Bank also accepted a corporate guarantee from United Breweries (Holdings), whose subsidiary was Kingfisher Airlines. The bank additionally secured a personal guarantee from Vijay Mallya. Strangely, Agarwal also initiated a process to expedite the process of rating Kingfisher while granting the loan.

Some of the loans disbursed by IDBI Bank were quickly transferred by Kingfisher Airlines to its accounts in other banks—Rs 169.62 crore to its account in Axis Bank, Rs 39 crore to its account in ICICI Bank and Rs 54 crore to its account in Bank of Baroda. This money was again quickly moved to other Kingfisher Airlines accounts elsewhere—many of them overseas. The money was hardly used for the purpose it had been sanctioned for. Most of it was used to pay aircraft rentals and for purchase of aircraft parts.

———

Agarwal was appointed the chairman of the Pension Fund Regulatory and Development Authority one-and-a-half years after his retirement. Batra—who officially initiated most of the Kingfisher proposals—is still with the bank. He has risen up the ranks and is now the deputy managing director. Bundellu also became deputy managing director at IDBI Bank before he retired.

Kingfisher was successful in getting a loan from IDBI Bank only in its second attempt. Three years earlier, in 2006, it had approached IDBI for funds to acquire aircraft. IDBI had refused to even consider its request. There was good reason for this: its past experience of dealing with Mallya had been bad. The two had tangoed in the case of lending to Mangalore Chemicals and Fertilizers that was run by Mallya.

The improper manner in which IDBI Bank lent to Kingfisher did not come to light until many years later. Only when banks started declaring Mallya a wilful defaulter did attention fall on IDBI. It came in for special scrutiny because it was the last commercial bank to extend credit to Kingfisher, after the airline had almost gone under. Many other public sector banks, led by SBI, had made huge loans to Kingfisher Airlines. But they could not be faulted. At the time they had lent to the airline, it had not been in a bad financial state.

By 2009-10, Kingfisher had accumulated debts of over Rs 7,000 crore. Losses were still piling up, and most bankers now thought there was no hope of reviving this 'non-performing asset'. In banking terminology, an NPA is an account from which there is no hope of being paid the interest owed, much less the principal. For the banker, loan recovery is of paramount importance, and he is very wary of writing off debts. Bankers always hope against hope that their loans will be returned, often persuading themselves to lend more funds to a badly performing debtor company. This is in the hope that the company will turn around and eventually repay them once it gets back on the rails.

Although the Kingfisher account was of such a category, the lenders, instead of declaring it an NPA, collectively agreed to lend it even more money. There was considerable debate among the senior bank managers over this, of course. Some of them bluntly said the writing on the wall was clear—there was no hope. But another set bought into the optimism projected by Mallya, who was cocksure that Kingfisher would make it. Ultimately, hope won, but the bankers insisted that Mallya must also give a personal guarantee for securing the loan. In that way he could be held personally liable if the company reneged on repayment. They thought this was sufficient caution.

In November 2010, the banks restructured Kingfisher's debts. The consortium of lenders led by SBI converted Rs 1,355 crore of Kingfisher's debts into equity, at a 60 per cent premium to the market price of the Kingfisher stock. The banks also extended the loan repayment period to nine years, with a two-year moratorium. By converting part of the loan into equity, the banks were essentially becoming stakeholders in Kingfisher Airlines. So, in the future, if the airline made profits, the banks would get their share. It also meant that as equity owners, the banks could directly sell off their Kingfisher shares if required.

By buying the shares at a premium, the banks were paying more than the market price. SBI and ICICI Bank bought compulsorily convertible debentures (CCD) that were converted into equity shares at a price of Rs 64.68 each on 31 March 2011. On this day, Kingfisher Airlines shares closed at Rs 39.50 on the Bombay Stock Exchange. It just goes to show how well Mallya used his powers of lobbying.

The banks also cut the interest rates and sanctioned a fresh loan. Answering a question in Parliament in 2011, Minister of State for Finance Namo Narain Meena said Kingfisher got the additional loans after providing extensive collaterals. This included Rs 538.59 crore by pledging Kingfisher House in Mumbai, Kingfisher Villa in Goa and hypothecation of helicopters. Another Rs 101.58 crore came through pledging of ground support and other equipment, Rs 22.43 crore through pledging of office computers of Kingfisher, Rs 13.39 crore through pledging of office equipment and Rs 33.35 crore through pledging of furniture and fixtures. An aircraft valued at Rs 107.77 crore was also pledged. But this was not all. Meena revealed that Kingfisher Airlines had pledged its brand to IDBI Bank for an estimated Rs 4,100 crore and Mallya had provided a personal guarantee of Rs 248.97 crore. United Breweries (Holdings) had also provided a corporate guarantee of Rs 1,601.43 crore for the loan.

The restructuring of loans to Kingfisher, as well as the additional loans made to it, was possible because of a change in RBI policy. The RBI, which had so far not allowed corporate debt restructuring for the aviation sector, permitted this from September 2010. Mallya had heavily lobbied for this change. After the global economic downturn that began in 2008-09, the airline sector started piling up losses, squeezed by shrinking demand that led to excess capacities. It is estimated that the cumulative debts of the Indian aviation sector stood at Rs 60,000 crore in March 2010. Of this, Rs 40,000 crore was due to Air India and Rs 7,000 crore due to Kingfisher Airlines. Banks were feeling the pinch badly.

SBI chairman O.P. Bhatt was quoted in a report by PTI in April 2010 as saying: 'Aviation sector is on an uptick. It is required to bring it out of stress.' As a result of all this, RBI liberalized norms for the sector, and Kingfisher was able to get financial accommodation from banks.

But this was to no avail because Kingfisher's performance showed no improvement. By the end of 2011 and early 2012, the lending banks had officially begun to declare Kingfisher an NPA. Now the banks started getting worried. The panic mounted as there were allegations that their loans to the Mallya airline had been diverted for other purposes. In a few months Kingfisher ceased operations and the banks were left high and dry. Banking sources say only ICICI Bank could negotiate its way out of trouble as it 'sold' its Rs 480 crore debt to a debt fund managed by SREI Infra Finance Limited.

On 1 March 2016, at a banking conference attended by top bankers, including SBI Chairman Arundhati Bhattacharya, ICICI Bank Chairman Chanda Kochhar and Axis Bank head Shikha Sharma, CBI Director Anil Sinha went hammer and tongs at them. He severely rebuked them for not filing complaints against Kingfisher Airlines for such huge defaults for years. 'This gave the company a huge berth to divert funds and destroy evidence,' an angry Sinha said. 'The message to the public is that the rich and the powerful are able to avoid consequences of cheating or fraud, while ordinary citizens are promptly booked. This undermines the faith of people in the rule of law, which has dangerous consequences in a democracy.' In spite of repeated requests, the banks did not file complaints with the CBI, and in the end the agency had to suo motu file cases against Kingfisher Airlines, he said.

Journalists hanging on the sidelines of the meeting that day approached the bankers about Sinha's accusations, but were met with evasive answers. Bhattacharya said that she would not answer questions about individual accounts, while Ashwini Kumar, the chairman of the Indian Banking Association, said the delay in filing complaints 'was not deliberate'. Sharma of Axis Bank said: 'As far as defaulters are concerned the client should have defaulted and we should be able to prove that these were wilful defaults. You have to go through a process, you have to give them a chance to hear the borrower because you cannot unilaterally declare them as wilful defaulters.'

The tardiness with which banks dealt with rogue borrowers was not just on account of the long procedures involved. Banks have been seeing a steep increase in their NPAs since the global slowdown of 2008. Many companies to which they had liberally lent in the boom years started going bust. The number of wilful defaulters at public sector banks increased from 5,554 to 7,686 between December 2012 and December 2015. The defaulters included big companies in the steel, power and infrastructure sectors, many of them possessing huge political clout. The statistics imply that these companies made every effort to keep banks at bay and ensure that action was not taken against them. Recourse to lengthy court procedures was one tactic. In this situation, Kingfisher appeared to be just one of the many recalcitrant clients that banks were dealing with.

But Kingfisher Airlines was still somewhat of a different case, if only because of its promoter, who continued to draw attention to himself with his high-octane parties even when his company was withering away. It shocked the public that Mallya was displaying his lavish lifestyle in such adverse circumstances, particularly when he was not paying employees their salary. Allegations that he was siphoning out money from the company to overseas destinations, and a rumour that one loan was used by Mallya to buy a stallion for his stud farm, brought him even more negative attention.

———

The first case in the Kingfisher matter was made by the CBI in the first week of October 2015, and related to the Rs 950 crore loan from IDBI Bank. The FIR was filed against Vijay Mallya, A. Raghunathan and unnamed officials of IDBI Bank. The FIR said IDBI officials had colluded with the promoters or directors or CFO of Kingfisher Airlines and sanctioned credit limits of Rs 950 crore in violation of bank norms, causing loss by their fraudulent act. The FIR was registered under sections relating to criminal conspiracy, criminal breach of trust by a public servant, and criminal misconduct.

The CBI then examined some of the accused in the FIR. Mallya himself was grilled by sleuths from the Bank Securities Fraud Cell at the CBI headquarters in Delhi on 10 December 2015. He was repeatedly asked about how he managed to secure a loan from IDBI in spite of the poor financials of his airline. He was also asked why he went to a bank that was not part of his original lending consortium. Usually, the practice is to approach one's original consortium partners for further loans. Mallya did not reveal much and was on guard, though his natural bravado was missing. Raghunathan was also interrogated, as were the IDBI officials—five of them. Ravi Nedungadi, who was the CFO of the UB Group for a long time, was also summoned by the CBI. These interrogations were followed by searches at the premises of Kingfisher Airlines in Mumbai, Bangalore and Goa. The Kingfisher Villa in Goa, where Mallya used to spend a lot of his time, was also searched. Incriminating documents were seized.

The CBI seems to have come to the initial conclusion that Kingfisher had spirited away US$200 million of its IDBI loans to 'tax haven' countries. Now, the CBI referred the case to the ED. Based on the CBI's FIR, the ED registered a case of money laundering under various sections of the Prevention of Money Laundering Act (PMLA). In parallel, the Serious Fraud Investigation Office (SFIO) that looks into violations of company law started probing the Kingfisher case.

News reports have carried some startling facts from their probe. Seventeen companies that lent money to Kingfisher had borrowed from banks. Instead of using the money themselves, they passed it on to Kingfisher. This means that banks have an even greater exposure to Kingfisher than was originally estimated. The SFIO has now given notice to these companies to explain their actions.

The SFIO is also examining whether the brand value of Rs 4,100 crore for Kingfisher Airlines assessed by multinational tax and advisory consultant Grant Thorton LLP was in order. Was the brand deliberately overvalued to allow Kingfisher Airlines to get more bank loans, which could subsequently be siphoned off? The SFIO has asked the consultant to justify why its assessment of Kingfisher Airlines' brand value was based on that of Kingfisher beer, a highly successful brand.

When the CBI alerted the ED, Mallya got alarmed. His disappearance from India is linked to the ED's involvement in the case. He successfully evaded summons from the ED to appear before the agency. On 9 April 2016, he (who had by now left India) informed the investigation officer on his case that he would not be able to appear before him because legal proceedings were on in the Supreme Court over settlement of bank loans taken by him and his company.

Upon this, the ED moved a special PMLA court, charging Mallya with siphoning off Rs 430 crore of the loan sanctioned to him by IDBI Bank and using it to acquire properties abroad. His lawyers contended before the court that this allegation was 'false and incorrect'. But the court rejected his pleas and issued a non-bailable warrant (NBW) against him on 19 April 2016.

Less than two months later, on 14 June 2016, the court also declared Mallya as a 'proclaimed offender' in the same case. This was after the ED had attached properties worth Rs 1,411 crore belonging to him and the UB Group. The properties attached included a bank balance of Rs 34 crore, a flat each in Bangalore and Mumbai (of 2,291 square feet and 1,300 square feet respectively), a 4.5-acre industrial plot in Chennai, a 28.75-acre coffee plantation in Kodagu (Coorg), and residential and commercial properties in UB City and Kingfisher Towers in Bangalore (8,410,279 square feet).

On 3 September, the ED made a larger attachment worth Rs 6,630 crore. This included a farmhouse belonging to Mallya in Mandwa, across the sea from Mumbai, worth Rs 20 crore, apartments and a mall in Bangalore worth Rs 800 crore, personal shares owned by Mallya in United Breweries Limited and United Spirits Limited worth Rs 3,000 crore, and his fixed deposits in a private bank. While serving the attachment notice, the ED said these assets were the proceeds generated out of the criminal activity of alleged default on bank loans. The ED notice also accused him of having criminally conspired with Kingfisher Airlines and UB (Holdings) to obtain funds from a consortium of banks.

Attachment of property by the ED does not mean the agency can take charge of it immediately. An attachment effectively means notice by the ED that these properties will be taken over. The actual takeover is legally possible only when the adjudicating authority of the ED permits this after hearing out the other party. This process could take up to a year, but in this case the proceedings have been fast. By November 2016, the special anti-money laundering court confirmed the attachment of Mallya's assets worth Rs 1,411 crore, paving the way for their takeover.

There are some reports that Mallya sold the coffee plantation before the ED could take it. If the new owner is able to prove his ownership, the attachment proceedings on the coffee estate would have to be reversed. The *Times of India*'s Bangalore edition reported on 14 January 2016 that Mallya had sold off his 315-acre coffee estate in Madikeri taluka of Kodagu. The sale was made to Mangalore-based educationist A. Janardhana Shetty. Apparently, Mallya had originally bought this property for his second wife Rekha but had abandoned it for vaastu reasons. Other newspaper reports suggest that the documents for the plantation could not be traced by the ED, although the agency was confident that the property deed would ultimately be found.

Mallya reacted strongly to the attachment of his property from his refuge in the UK, announcing that he was being 'deemed guilty without trial', and lambasted the investigators for leading a heavily biased investigation against him. He said,

'Purely civil matters such as loan recovery are being connected with criminal allegations without any basis whatsoever. It is disappointing that thousands of documents submitted by us and interrogation of several executives seem insufficient to convince them that that there was no wrongdoing.' Mallya's protestations are seen as part of his public relations strategy to shout from the rooftop that he is innocent and is being framed.

While all this was happening, the ED decided to launch proceedings to extradite Mallya from the UK in June. As a first step, it provided legal inputs and other documentation to Interpol, requesting it to issue a Red Corner Notice (RCN) against Mallya. An RCN from Interpol will set off a global alert for Mallya, who could be arrested at any airport anywhere in the world upon presenting himself before immigration officials. However, Interpol officials do not appear to be convinced by the ED's request and have asked for additional details. These were provided in early August 2016.

Sitting in the UK, Mallya is likely to use the local legal system to the hilt to prevent his extradition. A good public relations strategy will come in handy, which is why he has been playing the victim for a long time now. That the Indian investigating agencies have not been forceful in their approach does not help bring Mallya to book either.

————

The banks, though they had dragged their feet in filing timely complaints against Mallya, were quick to react when they realized that there was some chance of recovery of at least part of the money they had loaned to Kingfisher Airlines.

Around the time Mallya fled the country in early March 2016, the consortium of lenders to Kingfisher moved the Debt Recovery Tribunal (DRT) another time. The first case against Mallya had been filed at the DRT in Bangalore in 2013. Since then two dozen fresh petitions have been filed. It had so happened that in the last week of February 2016, United Spirits announced that Mallya had agreed to quit his position as chairman of the company and snap all ties with it. As part of what is called a 'sweetheart deal', Diageo, the majority owner of the company—agreed to pay Mallya a severance package of US$75 million (Rs 515 crore), US$40 million of it immediately and the remaining later.

Sensing an opportunity to recover some of their money, the consortium approached the DRT arguing that since Mallya had given personal guarantees when Kingfisher had taken a loan, the money that he was now getting belonged to the banks. They contended that the DRT must pass an order allowing them to take away this money. On 7 March 2016, the presiding officer of the Bangalore bench of the DRT, C.R. Benkanhalli, passed an order stalling the transaction of $75 million between Diageo and Mallya. However, barely four months later—on 13 July—the DRT was forced to describe its own order as infructuous. The amount of $40 million Mallya received had been transferred out of the country even before the order was passed. And the remaining $35 million was going to be paid to him only in the future.

The consortium now approached the DRT again on 30 June requesting a recovery certificate to start proceedings against Mallya to get their money from him, as the sum paid to him by Diageo was untraceable. But Diageo contended before the DRT that the court did not have any jurisdiction on offshore payments, thereby foreclosing any attachment of future payments. Diageo also let it be known that the payment had been made in February, before the banks had filed their petition.

While the DRT was unable to block Diageo's payment to Mallya, the consortium of bankers approached the Supreme Court, saying they were interested in recovering their dues. For this they wanted to obtain an idea of the assets held by him and his family. The court had on 8 April 2016 directed him to disclose all assets held by him and his family to his creditors. The list had to include moveable, immoveable, tangible and intangible assets owned by him, his wife and his children.

Mallya's lawyer initially opposed the order, arguing that his client was an NRI and that this disclosure was a violation of his privacy. He also contended that Mallya could be liable only to the extent of the personal guarantees he had given to the banks and a full disclosure would therefore not be in order. Foreign assets were not taken into consideration by banks while giving loans, the lawyer argued, and Mallya's wife (estranged from him) and his three children were overseas residents. Mallya complained that he was being subjected to a media trial. But the Supreme Court did not buy this argument.

On 27 April 2016, Mallya provided in a sealed cover the details of all assets held by him to the court. This was later passed over to the consortium of banks, which moved the Supreme Court on 14 July 2016 to say that the liquor baron had not fully disclosed details of his assets. Attorney General Mukul Rohatgi told the court, 'Mallya has not fully complied with the directions of the court.' He described Mallya as a fugitive of justice. 'The bank's money was the people's money and thus they have the right to examine Mallya's assets,' said Rohatgi. The banks also complained that the details provided by Mallya were vague and that in some cases there were significant omissions. For instance, there was no reference to the money he had received from Diageo, and no mention of another Rs 2,000 crore cash deal he had entered into. This was contempt of court, the lawyers argued. The Supreme Court agreed, issuing a contempt notice to Mallya on 26 July 2016.

Early that July, SBI Chairman Arundhati Bhattacharya said the bank was willing to make a one-time settlement with Mallya. This revelation came when a thirty-member joint parliamentary panel set up to suggest changes to the present debt recovery laws asked the SBI chief for her views on the matter. The *Times of India*, on 4 July 2016, reported that the SBI chief had told the panel that the bank was willing to settle if Mallya was ready to repay the outstanding principal amount along with some (she did not specify how much) interest and legal fees already spent by the bank in pursuing the case against him. The SBI boss said Mallya had put up 'some conditions', which were not acceptable to the bank. She did not specify what they were but told the MPs the bank was 'not insisting on payment of interest upon interest'. In normal practice, the liability of a debtor who does not pay interest on time mounts because banks want interest payments on unpaid interest, as well as interest payments on that part of the loan that remains unpaid.

Mallya had earlier—in April 2016—agreed to pay up Rs 4,000 crore, which he claimed was the amount borrowed from banks. The payment would be made by September that year, he said. But the banks rejected this offer, firstly because it was too low and then because he was abroad. They had suggested that he should be in the country for easier negotiations. His lawyers argued that their client could very well carry on his negotiations over video-conferencing and phone calls. At a later stage, he revised his offer to Rs 4,850 crore, including a component of Rs 150 crore to cover the banks' legal and other expenses. His lawyers have also pressed the point that the liquor baron was a defaulter but certainly not a wilful defaulter.

According to the banks, Mallya and Kingfisher Airlines borrowed a total of Rs 6,963 crore from seventeen banks. Finance Minister Arun Jaitley told Parliament on 21 July 2016 that Kingfisher owed Rs 9,091.4 crore, including interest, to banks as on 30 November 2015. There was a gross mismatch between how much Mallya thinks he owes the banks and how much the banks say his debts to them are. In such a situation a negotiated settlement seems very difficult, though both parties claim they are keen on it.

Mallya then changed tack and adopted the strategy that offence is the best defence. At a hearing at the DRT on 25 July 2016, his lawyers came up with a new argument: he was not liable to pay a single paisa to the banks on account of Kingfisher because the banks that lent money to the airline had themselves breached the terms and conditions of the debt restructuring agreement, leading to needless damages to Kingfisher's business. They said the agreement was drawn up so that the airline business could continue in the interests of the economy, something stated explicitly in a letter written by the SBI to the RBI at that time. The lawyers claimed SBI chairman Pratip Chaudhuri's statement that Kingfisher had turned into an NPA had sent the airline's share prices plummeting.

But it is not the banks alone that Mallya owes money to. The service tax department raised a demand on Kingfisher Airlines and has approached the courts. It claims that the defunct airline owes as much as Rs 535 crore to it. This is the sum that Kingfisher had collected from passengers as service tax on tickets (when it was flying) but failed to deposit to the department. To get its dues, the department had also seized some planes of Kingfisher. But an attempt to auction them was not successful. One of the seized planes is Mallya's personal jet, a 225-seater A-319 that was converted into a 25-seater with a bar, a bedroom and a conference hall. There was only one interested party at the auction in mid-June and the bid offered was lower than the reserve price. The department is planning another auction to sell the plane.

The income tax department says that tax of Rs 679.80 crore is leviable on Kingfisher Airlines. The department has written to United Breweries to 'create a charge' against this, which means that any dividend, director's commission or other payments due to Mallya would be withheld by the company and given to the government. United Breweries was, meanwhile, been ordered by the DRT to withhold any dividend payable to him for the financial year 2015-16. Accordingly, the company withheld his dividend of Rs 9.33 crore for that year. His director's commission of Rs 1.61 crore was also withheld.

In January 2017, the DRT allowed the consortium of banks to initiate the process of recovering Rs 6,203 crore along with interest (chargeable at 11.5 per cent) from Mallya and his companies. A few days afterwards, the CBI moved in to make the first arrests in the case. All the IDBI bankers involved in sanctioning the controversial loan to Kingfisher Airlines were put behind bars; they were Yogesh Agarwal, B.K. Batra, O.V. Bundellu, S.K.V. Srinivasan and R.S. Sridhar. Kingfisher Airlines' CFO A. Raghunathan and three other executives were also arrested. In early February 2017, the CBI filed a charge sheet in the case accusing Mallya and his associates of diverting a large part of their loan for purposes other than for which it was sanctioned. Part of the loan was used to pay the lease rents for a private jet for Mallya's use, part of it to square off a past loan taken by Kingfisher Airlines from IDBI, and part of it to pay past dues to the income tax department. Payment of dues to the I-T department neither formed part of its loan appraisal note nor was mentioned anywhere in the request letters seeking the note.

13

The Mallya Empire Falls Apart

EARLY IN JULY 2013, Diageo completed its takeover of United Spirits Limited, eight months after it had announced it would. The original deadline was March 2013, but a number of regulatory issues delayed the acquisition. The Competition Commission of India (CCI) and the SEBI sought more details on how the deal would affect the balance of ownership in the liquor industry in India before giving it the green signal. This was to be expected, as Diageo was the world's largest spirits manufacturer and its entry into the Indian market had the potential to skew the industry. The final regulatory clearance came only in June 2013.

A further delay was caused by a petition filed by Kingfisher Airlines to wind up UB (Holdings) Limited. UB (Holdings) had given corporate guarantees worth Rs 8,925.86 crore to Kingfisher Airlines' creditors. Originally, Diageo had announced it would acquire a 53.5 per cent stake in United Spirits Limited (USL), but in the end Diageo could garner only 25.02 per cent of its equity. However, it did become its largest shareholder—and officially the promoter of USL responsible for managing the company.

Vijay Mallya had built the company from 1983, from a liquor division of United Breweries producing 3 million cases of spirits to an enterprise churning out 120 million cases in 2012. Naturally, he had a strong emotional connect with the business. But he had to sell off because he had no other option. He was in a bad way—or so it seemed—because of Kingfisher Airlines, and he could only survive by selling the family silver to get some cash to bail himself out. But the company was his life, and he wished to continue as its non-executive chairman. Diageo had assented: after all, this was a man who knew better than anybody else the company and its market. His presence would bring them helpful tips and give a sense of continuity to the managers who would run the company, a large number of them being old-timers from the Mallya stable.

But along with continuity there had to be change too. So a new management was put in place. The Mallya appointees were removed from the board of directors at USL and replaced with Diageo's own representatives and eminent public persons of its choosing. They included the former chief secretary of Karnataka, Sudhakar Rao, and the former Mumbai police commissioner D. Sivanandhan, who were inducted as independent directors. For some time the new promoters continued with Mallya's earlier managing director, Ashok Capoor, an old hand at the company from the McDowell days. Later, he was replaced by Anand Kripalu, an FMCG professional who had spent considerable time in Unilever India.

The Bangalore edition of the *Times of India* reported on 13 August 2013: 'Top UB group executives and close aides of the troubled billionaire Vijay Mallya who were parked on the payrolls of United Spirits Limited have been shifted out with Diageo tightening the leash over India's largest distiller. No slots for Mallya's bulge bracket executives including some involved with the grounded Kingfisher Airlines.' Some of the executives named in the report were UB Group president and CFO Ravi Nedungadi, UB (Holdings) MD Harish Bhatt, Kingfisher Airlines' CFO A. Raghunathan, and its company secretary and chief legal officer, Bharat Raghavan.

With Mallya's men out of the way, the company secrets that had been kept under wraps for so long now started tumbling out. The statutory auditors' heavily qualified report noted that United Spirits had given out loans to Kingfisher and to UB (Holdings) that had not been returned, neither their principal nor interest. The auditor also reported that USL had received notices from some claimants who alleged that they had advanced loans to Kingfisher Airlines on the basis of agreements by which USL had provided a lien on certain investments as security. The claimants were demanding Rs 79 crore against Kingfisher's default on repayment of their loans. Seeing the statutory auditors' report, the new management of USL commissioned a special audit that confirmed the conclusions of the report.

Although Diageo had done a due diligence of sorts before buying into USL, they were now realizing that all was not right with their new acquisition. In view of the auditors' report, the new management scrutinized all the company documents. They discovered that USL had given many loans, advances and deposits to UB (Holdings) without any collateral. These loans, made in tranches that added up to Rs 1,337 crore, were therefore unsecured loans. UB (Holdings) was in no position to pay back the loans. So USL, on 3 July

2013, entered into a fresh agreement with UB (Holdings). The latter would return all the money that it had borrowed over eight years; but there would be a moratorium period of six years.

Diageo was still not satisfied; it wanted to find out what exactly was wrong in the company. After all, the statutory auditors, until 2011, were the internationally reputed PricewaterhouseCoopers (PwC). To play it safe, the new company management thought it would make sense for the company to be audited by a foreign auditor. The task fell on the London branch of PwC. Simultaneously, Ernst & Young was also assigned the same duty. After receiving the reports, USL found—and later publicly announced—that the erstwhile promoters had diverted Rs 1,225 crore to entities linked to Mallya.

Now it was no longer tenable for Mallya to continue as the chairman of the company. He was asked to step down after an emergency board meeting in April 2015, but the supersized ego of the 'king of good times' had been pricked. He said he was not aware of the inquiry. So far as he was concerned, all transactions made by United Spirits had been legal, above-board, and approved by the board of the company and its shareholders, he said. Moreover, the auditors of the time, the Bangalore branch of PwC, had found nothing amiss in these deals, he said, pointing out that Diageo itself had done its due diligence of USL before acquiring the company. So how was it that nothing wrong was found earlier? Mallya also asserted that a director of a company cannot be asked to go by the board of directors. It was only the shareholders of the company who could vote him out. He was still a 4 per cent shareholder in USL. At its annual general meeting in September 2015, he insisted he would chair the meeting and address the shareholders.

What followed were months of tussle between the new owners of USL and Mallya, the latter insisting he was guilty of nothing, and that he had not been named personally in the adverse reports; it was wrong to ask him to step down just a day after the audit reports were submitted; and if he did so, it would be tantamount to admission of guilt on his part. He also hinted that if he had been told he had been chairman of the company for too long and should step down to make way for new blood he would have agreed. He pointed out that the contractual agreements that the new purchasers had entered into made it mandatory for them to continue with him. At the same time, he hinted that he was ready for a clean break if USL and he could arrive at a mutual settlement, and as soon as possible.

It was after this that USL decided to give him a severance package of $75 million and get rid of him. On 25 February 2016, USL announced that he had quit as chairman and non-executive director of the company. The compensation given to him came with a five-year non-compete, non-interference and standstill condition. This meant that Mallya could not start another liquor company nor buy into United Spirits directly or through his associates, nor meddle in the company's affairs. (But this agreement is not applicable in the UK, the country Mallya fled to four days after stepping down.) USL also agreed not to press charges against him for the irregularities found in the company's books by the auditors. In addition it agreed to recognize him as the founder-emeritus of the company, as an acknowledgement of his role in United Spirits.

Mallya also wrangled another deal: Diageo extended

the sponsorship of the Force India team, of which he is the principal and part owner, for five seasons under its Smirnoff brand. Each year's sponsorship costs $15 million.

After Mallya's exit, the directors elected Mahendra Kumar Sharma as the chairman of USL. A former vice-chairman of Hindustan Unilever and currently also non-executive chairman of ICICI Bank, he is one of the top corporate law experts in the country.

USL had agreed not to press charges against Mallya, but additional inquiries into the books of accounts of USL (ordered after the irregularities detected in the audit made public in April 2015) revealed further evidence of alleged wrongdoings in the company. These additional inquiries were done by forensic experts, who claimed there were fund diversions of Rs 1,225.30 crore from USL for the review period October 2010 to July 2014. Of this, overseas diversions to entities affiliated to or associated with Mallya accounted for Rs 311.80 crore. The overseas beneficiaries, the additional investigations revealed, included Force India, Formula One, Watson Ltd, Continental Administrative Services, Modall Securities, Ultra Dynamics and Lombard Wall Corporate Services Inc. This evidence was brought before the board of directors of USL on 9 July 2016 and immediately notified to the stock exchanges. The company said the 'board further noted that the mutual release agreed to with Dr Mallya announced on February 25, 2016 does not extend to the matter arising out of the additional enquiries.' The statement also pointed out that 'only a court/regulatory body would be in a position to make a final determination about fault and culpability'.

Meanwhile, USL had to provide for these newly detected losses in their balance sheet. This meant the company had to show losses, even though its operations were robust. Technically, it became a sick company under Indian law: the company's net worth (which is defined as profits plus reserves, reserves being undistributed profits not paid out as dividend) had been eroded by 52 per cent in the previous four financial years.

USL sold Whyte & Mackay, which had been acquired by Mallya a few years ago. Though the sale was done to overcome the competition laws in the UK, the proceeds of the sale (£408 million) came in handy to defray a part of the huge loan that had been taken by Mallya to buy this company in 2007.

At the end of August 2016, USL auctioned thirty of his vintage cars to recover some of its losses. The cars were part of his collection, but USL must have figured out that they were actually owned by the company. How much the company made out of the sales is not clear, but among the cars put on the block were a 1903 Humber, a Bentley Turbo and a British-manufactured Lancaster. News reports said the Humber went for Rs 1 crore and the Lancaster for nearly Rs 2 crore. A USL spokesperson said: 'Proceeds from monetizing non-core assets will be used to pare debts.'

———

Mallya more or less controlled his empire through United Breweries (Holdings) Limited, a company in which he and corporations controlled by him hold over 52.34 per cent of the shares. But he is in imminent danger of losing this company too, with eight banks having filed 'winding up' petitions against it in court. The problem for UB (Holdings) is that it stood guarantee for many of the borrowings of Kingfisher Airlines.

UB (Holdings) is also the original company of the group and was started over a hundred years ago in 1857 to brew and sell beer. Over the years the brewing activities were shifted to another company, United Breweries, while United Breweries (Holdings) became a holding company and the investment arm of the group. It holds control over an assortment of Mallya's businesses. It owns the trademarks of Pegasus and Kingfisher. Its other activities are trading in leather shoes, real estate development, sports, infrastructure, international trade, branded consumer goods and polymers. The company also trades beer, and makes money through export of Kingfisher beer to South-East Asia. Mallya had wanted this company to leverage his valuable land bank and forge a fortune from it. Companies such as City Maintenance Corporation, a real estate company, are grouped under UB (Holdings).

UB (Holdings) owns twenty-five companies; and of course it owns shares in United Breweries (overseeing the beer business), United Sprits (overseeing the liquor business in good times) and Kingfisher Airlines. UB (Holdings) is the only company in which Siddharth was also a director—a non-executive, non-independent director. But in March 2016 he resigned so as to keep himself at arm's length from the company.

How closely Mallya managed this company is clear from the appointment of his secretary in his London office, Daljit Mahal, to the board of UB (Holdings). The ostensible reason was the requirement for female representation on the board. Like all other companies in the Mallya stable, UB (Holdings) is also neck-deep in problems as a result of the state of affairs at Kingfisher Airlines. The accounts of the company for 2014-15 were heavily qualified by the auditors: they noted that UB (Holdings) had extended corporate guarantees of Rs 8,707.2 crore in favour of lenders, lessors and creditors of Kingfisher Airlines. The beneficiaries of these guarantees have now invoked them and recovery proceedings are on, the auditors noted. It was also reported that UB (Holdings) made investments equivalent of Rs 255.8 crore in subsidiaries and an associate company, which have declined in value since, and whose depreciation has not been provided in its books. The auditor also pointed out that certain subsidiaries of UB (Holdings) collectively owed the company Rs 75.4 crore. This has significantly eroded the net worth of the company, impairing recovery of the money. Further, a bank had unilaterally encashed Rs 36.7 crore of fixed deposits of UB (Holdings) lying with it. It had deducted this amount against claims it had on Kingfisher Airlines. The audit report also said the books of accounts of UB (Holdings) showed it was owed Rs 847.5 crore by a financial firm. It was clear that the accounts of UB (Holdings) were in a mess, an indicator that the floating of Kingfisher Airlines had landed it in a lot of trouble.

Though Mallya had wanted to leverage the real estate controlled by UB (Holdings), he had kept his properties undervalued. Perhaps he did not want his creditors to know how much his assets were really worth. However, this undervaluation did not escape the auditors' eye. UB (Holdings) had to obtain 'a fair market valuation' of its assets, based on the valuation report of an independent, approved valuation agency at the end of March 2014. This resulted in an appreciation in valuation to the tune of Rs 750. 85 crore.

This amount has now been accounted for in the revaluation reserve of the company.

Even for the year 2015-16, the annual statement of accounts was heavily qualified by the auditors. UB (Holdings) has declared a small loss for the year, but the auditors have said the losses would have been much higher had the company taken into account its various liabilities; they had not been recorded in the annual statement of income and expenditures. Now UB (Holdings) is also locked in a dispute with USL, which has invoked the arbitration clause to recover Rs 1,337.41 crore, plus the interest on it. Arbitration proceedings have commenced in the matter. On its part, UB (Holdings) has started arbitration to settle its dispute with the Zuari Agro group over its agreement with them for Mangalore Chemicals & Fertilizers.

UB (Holdings) has also initiated legal proceedings against the banks that have been taking over its assets in lieu of unpaid loans by the Mallya company. UB (Holdings) has moved court against SBI Cap, the trustee of the consortium of banks that have taken possession of Kingfisher Villa in Goa. UB (Holdings) has challenged this possession.

Analysts say UB (Holdings) was always poorly managed, and in a way that is not fathomable at all by the lay person. Investment analyst Luke Varghese, writing in Equitymaster.com on the company's financial results of 2010-11, noted that the subsidiaries of UB (Holdings) excelled each other in 'absurdities' and that some of them, like Rigby International, had zero turnover but were yet shown to have recorded a loss! The company's reserves were negative, which meant its capital base had been totally eroded. This was the case too with UBHL (BVI), a group company floated in the British

Virgin Islands, which had negative reserves, zero turnover and no revenue. UB (Holdings) appeared to be totally devoid of any corporate governance, Varghese noted. Writing on the financial results of 2011-12, Varghese remarked on the 'unbecoming margins' churned out by the company: 'The major investments of the group companies do not yield a farthing but the promoter family, which has the majority shares, is not complaining.' He noted that the company had loaned out large sums to subsidiaries. The loans were not returned on time, and to fund this extravagance UB (Holdings) borrowed large sums!

———

Even United Breweries, the company through which Vijay Mallya operates his beer empire, may well slip out of his hands. Since the Kingfisher debacle began, the company already has for all practical purposes. In 2009, the third largest beer company in the world, the Dutch conglomerate Heineken, entered into an equal joint venture agreement with Mallya, each party holding a 37.3 per cent stake in United Breweries. Both became the promoters of the company and agreed to jointly run it. Heineken also got the right to three board seats on United Breweries, including that of the finance director and the CFO. Although relations between the management of Heineken and Mallya have been very good, the Dutch company's equity has subsequently risen, as it has picked up UB shares that banks have been offloading. Today the Dutch company is a 44 per cent owner of United Breweries. A report in the *Times of India* by Boby Kurian said this freed Heineken from the 'equal shareholding and joint management clause'.

The stage is set for Heineken to claim management control over United Breweries. However, it is in no hurry to make this claim, given the perception that United Breweries will eventually fall into its lap as Mallya may not have any assets left to repay his loans. The only way he can tide over his troubles is to offload his shares in United Breweries to pay off his debts. His shares will fetch a good price as the company has been notching up a sterling performance. Even within the company, the staff no longer perceive it as a Mallya concern even though he is still the chairman.

'I joined the company recently. Although the top managers are from Mallya's time, I was told that this company is a Heineken enterprise now,' says a newly hired junior manager.

Many of the directors on the board of the company are still Mallya men. These include Ravi Nedungadi. Even Kiran Mazumdar-Shaw, a personal friend of Mallya's, is still on the board. The managing director of the company, Shekhar Ramamurthy, an IIT Delhi and IIM Calcutta alumnus, has worked in the company since 1989. Govind Iyengar, the company secretary, is also a Mallya-time executive, a company employee since 2001. Informed sources say that Heineken being a family-owned, family-run enterprise, its management style is different from that of a professionally managed company. Since Mallya has personal associations with the bosses of Heineken, they will allow him to continue until 'push comes to shove', say sources.

At the company's last annual general meeting on 7 September 2016, shareholders asked if it was possible that

Mallya had stopped being the chairman. Their apprehension was that the ED's attachment of his properties would make him ineligible for the post. But Chugh Yoginder Pal, who was chairing the meeting, said the company had sought legal opinion from a former chief justice of the Supreme Court who had said Mallya could continue in his post. Vijay Mallya would continue to be the chairman of the company. His message as chairman was read out to the shareholders that day. Expressing displeasure over the non-inclusion of alcohol in the new GST (Goods and Services Tax) dispensation, he said the company would rework its product portfolio and include new launches; increase its capacity, either of its existing breweries or by acquisition; and build new ones. He also said the company was in talks with state governments about taxes on alcoholic beverages.

United Breweries is performing well financially. For the fiscal year 2015-16, the company had a turnover of Rs 4,825.17 crore and net profit of Rs 297.87 crore, bettering the previous year's figures. In 2016-17, it transferred Rs 29.5 crore from its profits to the general reserve. In 2014-15, the turnover of the company was Rs 4,692.29 crore and its net profit Rs 259.53 crore. Due to the presence of Heineken and the finance director chosen by them, the company's annual report did not carry tough qualifications from the auditors.

Heineken came into United Breweries in an indirect way. As recorded earlier in the book, Mallya read the signs of globalization early on and inducted Edinburgh-based brewer Scottish & Newcastle (S&N) as a 17.5 per cent equity partner in UB as early as December 2004. A year later, S&N raised its equity to 37.5 per cent, as pre-arranged. It appointed a CFO— Lesley Jackson—from its own stable. The existing Mallya-appointed CFO, P.A. Murali, was sent to United Spirits along with some other officials. Mallya got Rs 940 crore from the deal, which he presumably invested in Kingfisher Airlines. Three years later, in 2008-09, Heineken bought over S&N automatically via ownership of United Breweries. The takeover, however, had to be approved by the CCI.

———

If Mallya were to lose control of both United Breweries and United Breweries (Holdings), he would lose total control of the core of his empire. Losing UB (Holdings) would take longer because of the wide variety of businesses carried out by it. Although some of the property controlled by the company has already been attached by the ED, he has put up a tough legal battle that may drag on for years. He could also try to sell off some of the real estate in the control of UB (Holdings) to settle his debts with banks. This would not be easy, of course, because the process is now being overseen by the Supreme Court. The element of criminality arising from diversion of cash overseas would also complicate the process. Such a charge is not easy to prove in court, but Mallya's is hardly going to be a simple case of the returning of cash borrowed from banks. The investigating agencies don't have a fix on the entire details of the cash that is alleged to be stashed away by Mallya in foreign lands, though they say they have made a lot of findings lately.

There is still another company that Mallya owns, and hopes he will not lose control of. The Mendocino Brewery Company in California is 68 per cent owned by Mallya. He is the chairman of the company too. The company brews craft beer and ale. More importantly, it has rights to market Kingfisher beer. United Breweries of America Inc. (UBA), a subsidiary of UB (Holdings), holds 24 per cent of Mendocino. From the filings before the Securities and Exchange Commission (SEC) of the US, it appears that UBA has made fourteen separate advances of money to Mendocino, which the latter has not been able to pay back and has sought extension for repayment. Sleuths from the ED suspect that these advances could be a conduit for siphoning away money. The suspicion has arisen because Mendocino, which was a beneficiary of these fund infusions, now seems to be, according to local press reports in California, in 'dire financial straits'. The press reports, quoting filings made by Mendocino's management to the SEC, have said the brewery could fold up if it does not come to receive a promised $1 million loan 'from chairman of the board and indirect majority stakeholder, industrialist Vijay Mallya'. Since that infusion is a near impossibility, Mendocino Brewery's shutdown is not an impossibility either.

Afterword

SIXTY IS THE NORMAL age of retirement in India. When Vijay Mallya turned sixty in December 2015, he had expressed a wish to spend more time with his children, hinting that he would take a back seat at work. But not many believed him. His personality, they felt, was not attuned that way. Work was not just an activity but part of his very lifestyle.

'Anyway, work is a fun thing for him and the two (work and life) cannot be divorced so far as he is concerned,' says an old associate of his.

But right now Mallya is walking his talk—though not by choice. He has lost most of his businesses and is living in London, virtually as a fugitive. He cannot get out of the UK, and those who have work to do with him must travel to London to meet him. This is what his close associates at UB (Holdings) and United Breweries have been doing—regularly travelling to the UK to confabulate with him and get papers signed. (The company secretary of UB Holdings, Kaushik Majumdar, travelled to London from Bangalore in August 2016 to get the annual results signed by Mallya.)

Most Indians are sceptical of the country's system of

justice; they swear nothing will happen to Mallya, and that after some time everybody will forget about his misdeeds (which will take a long time to prove, anyway). They also feel it will not be easy for Indian authorities to surmount the British legal system and get him extradited. But Mallya himself is on tenterhooks. He may have friends and acquaintances across the spectrum whom he has obliged in many ways. But he knows many of them are just fair-weather associates and could desert him. The signals being sent out from India do not bode well for him either. The Supreme Court in early September 2016 declined permission to industrialist Ravi Ruia—vice-chairman of the Essar group, charged by the CBI over alleged corruption involving the sale of 2G spectrum—to travel abroad, saying it didn't want to take a chance any more: 'It is like once bitten twice shy. We had passed a wrong order allowing a person to go abroad and he is not coming back. We don't want to commit the same mistake again.'

Although the court did not identify who it was talking about, the reference was lost on no one. 'Mallya's escape is a blot on the government, which will now be doubly conscious about how it deals with him,' says a senior BJP leader. Legal experts say it will be very difficult for Mallya to get a favourable order from the Supreme Court.

Mallya's escape has provided detractors of the government a good opportunity to take potshots at it. Rahul Gandhi, vice-president of the Congress—under whose government Mallya got all the bank loans—has been frequently attacking the Centre over the Mallya fiasco. While campaigning in UP in early September 2016 for the state elections, he said: 'When farmers leave with cots, they are called thieves, but when industrialists run away with Rs 9,000 crore, they are called defaulters.' He was hitting back at the Modi government in retaliation for the ridicule the Congress came in for when, after its rural rally the previous day, farmers who had been provided cots to sit on had made away with them. Mallya fears the Modi government, in a bid to erase the embarrassment caused by his flight, will strongly pressure the British authorities for his repatriation.

That Mallya is living on hope is clear from his tweets. His tagline says it all: '"Life isn't about waiting for the storm to pass. It's about learning to dance in the rain": Vivian Greene.' Nothing from his tweets indicates his present misfortunes—perhaps his lawyers have advised silence on the matter. Even his tweets on sporting events are confined to his teams' activities. He did not comment on other sporting events of national interest such as the Olympic wins of P.V. Sindhu or Sakshi Malik.

Perhaps Mallya wonders what he can now bequeath to his son Siddharth. It is not unusual for fathers to worry about what they will leave for their children. Siddharth is unlike Vijay as far as business is concerned. Mallya has been quite an indulgent father, keeping Siddharth away from the hard life. In the process, the son has not shown an inclination to do business. Siddharth, who prefers to be called Sid, is mainly interested in acting. (He once dated Bollywood actress Deepika Padukone.) He appeared in a movie, *Brahman Naman*, produced in London, and will soon appear in another, called *Homecoming*. He has now set his sights on Hollywood.

The only enterprises of his father's that he showed interest in were the football club, Mohun Bagan, and the cricket team,

Royal Challengers Bangalore. He was also a judge on the Kingfisher talent hunt for models. From his tweets, it would appear that he was actively engaged in running the Barbados Trident team owned by his father in the Caribbean. He also followed the Formula One races very closely in 2016.

It is interesting to imagine Mallya sitting in England and thinking about Warren Hastings, the first English governor general of Bengal and India. Mallya was a member of Hastings House in his school. Hastings had to face impeachment proceedings in the British parliament for allegedly misusing his powers and amassing wealth while serving in India. It was a long-drawn-out impeachment that went on from 1788 to 1795, at the end of which he was acquitted. Although he lived in style throughout the time the procedure was on, he was financially ruined and mentally exhausted when it ended. He had to kneel before the House of Lords every time he was summoned and even when he was acquitted, something he found 'ignominious' because this was inflicted as a 'punishment even before conviction'.

Historians have remarked that Hastings was not an unreasonable man and had worked hard to set up systems in the part of India ruled by the British. Moreover, he was not greedy and had made little money compared with his contemporaries like Lord Clive and other officials of the East India Company. In fact, Hastings had fallen victim to the machinations of his rivals who were jealous of him. This happened at a time when every official of the East India Company who returned from India was labelled a Nabob for the fortunes he amassed, usually through rapacious activities. It was easy then for public opinion to turn against him. While returning from India, he did know he would be attacked in the press and in parliament, but he had not expected the matter to linger on and subject him to such a long tribulation.

Perhaps, Mallya too wonders how long his trial will last and prays it will come to a quick close.

Acknowledgements

IT IS BELIEVED THAT 99 per cent of the intelligence of the Central Intelligence Agency in the US comes from published information and only 1 per cent comprises information that the premier agency procures from human intelligence (Humint). This serves to drive home the point that much of what we think is exclusive information is already available in the public domain but it takes skill and patience to cull out and compile the relevant information from a variety of documents.

A large volume of the material for this book came from diverse publicly available sources. This includes Mallya companies' annual reports that have to be filed to the statutory authorities and put in the public domain. Added to this were declarations that the companies had to make to the Bombay Stock Exchange and the National Stock Exchange. Some information about US subsidiaries was also obtained from the US Securities and Exchange Commission. All these sources provided deep insights into the working of the group. An internal group magazine called *Pegasus* that came out for over ten years, and which is in the public domain, proved to be a good source of information about the company's internal perspectives and plans.

Newspapers like the *Times of India*, *Economic Times*, *Mint*, *Hindustan Times*, *Indian Express* and the *Mumbai Mirror* threw up important information that I drew upon to write *Kingfizzer*. For a longer-term perspective, magazines like *India Today* (especially some of its older issues) and other business magazines like *Business India* and *Business World* came in handy.

Humint, which journalists and writers call sources, is very crucial for information. I spoke with dozens of people, including present and past Mallya group company managers and journalists and bankers who had the chance to observe how he and his companies operated. Many of them have been quoted by name in the book while some have preferred to remain anonymous. Officials of government agencies investigating Mallya's affairs also did not want to be named and were discreet.

At least two former senior executives of Mallya's companies provided information that threw light on how he did business. However, they were not willing to be quoted nor was there any documentary corroborative evidence. Thus, this information could not be used.

I must thank Krishan Chopra, Publisher at HarperCollins, for reposing his faith in me and overseeing this project. Two bright editors, Kripa Raman and Siddhesh Inamdar, did a fine job of editing the manuscript and thanks are due to them.

I have to express my appreciation of Shilpa Sivakumaran, who read the draft manuscript before I sent it to the publishers.

I fell critically ill in the middle of this project. I have to thank my wife Swati Sucharita for nursing me back to health and bearing with my mood swings. She also read through some of the chapters and provided valuable feedback.

In the end, the mandatory declaration: I alone am responsible for any mistakes that may have crept in.

Select Bibliography

1. The Beginning of the End

TNN, 'Vijay Mallya at his country home near London? Top priority is to make him return, *Times of India*, 10 March 2016, http://timesofindia.indiatimes.com/india/Vijay-Mallya-at-his-country-home-near-London-Top-priority-is-to-make-him-return-says-govt/articleshow/51338781.cms

Ankur Sharma, 'How Vijay Mallya flew to London via Delhi', *Mail Today*, 11 March 2016, http://indiatoday.intoday.in/story/vijay-mallyas-great-escape-via-delhi/1/617331.html

PTI, 'Vijay Mallya says he paid $100 to acquire CPL franchise Barbados Tridents', *Times of India*, 11 April 2016, http://timesofindia.indiatimes.com/top-stories/Vijay-Mallya-says-he-paid-100-to-acquire-CPL-franchise-Barbados-Tridents/articleshow/51779793.cms

Cricbuzz Staff, 'Vijay Mallya acquired Barbados Trident for just 100 USD', Cricbuzz.com, 11 April 2016, http://www.cricbuzz.com/cricket-news/79240/vijay-mallya-acquired-barbados-trident-for-just-100-usd

P.R. Sanjai, 'Vijay Mallya firms diverted funds up to Rs 1,225 crore: United Spirits', *Mint*, 9 July 2016, http://www.livemint.com/Companies/jKsodD2JDS70UI0lxmCisL/Inquiry-finds-fund-diversion-of-Rs1225-cr-by-Vijay-Mallyas.html

FP Staff, 'Mallya was in RS on 1 March, he left on 2nd: Here are the pores in system that let him go', FirstPost.com, 10 March 2016, http://www.firstpost.com/business/mallya-was-in-rs-on-1-march-he-left-on-2nd-here-are-the-pores-that-let-him-leave-2667244.html

PTI, 'Vijay Mallya skips ED again; seeks time till May', *Mint*, 9 April 2016, http://www.livemint.com/Politics/LEmqfubpQeolJdF4UtQgkO/Vijay-Mallya-skips-ED-again-seeks-time-till-May.html

Deeptiman Tiwary, 'First lookout notice against Vijay Mallya was a mistake: CBI', *Indian Express*, 12 March 2016, http://indianexpress.com/article/india/india-news-india/first-lookout-notice-against-vijay-mallya-was-a-mistake-cbi/

2. Kingfisher Airlines: The Take-off and the Crash

R. Jagannathan, 'Lesson to learn from Vijay Mallya's hubris-driven fall: don't bet the farm', FirstPost.com, 1 April 2014, http://www.firstpost.com/business/lesson-to-learn-from-vijay-mallyas-hubris-driven-fall-dont-bet-the-farm-1981983.html/amp

Anirban Chowdhury, 'Kingfisher Airlines owes 3,000 employees Rs 300 crore in salary', *Economic Times*, 10 March 2016, http://economictimes.indiatimes.com/industry/transportation/airlines-/-aviation/kingfisher-airlines-owes-3000-employees-rs-300-crore-in-salary/articleshow/51336437.cms

Saurabh Sinha, 'Kingfisher Airlines's 15 leased planes may land in scrapyards', *Times of India*, 8 April 2013, http://timesofindia.indiatimes.com/business/india-business/Kingfisher-Airliness-15-leased-planes-may-land-in-scrapyards/articleshow/19436669.cms

3. Vittal Mallya: The Reclusive Founding Father

'Vittal Mallya: Empire Builder', *India Today*, 31 July 1982, http://indiatoday.intoday.in/story/vittal-mallya-the-industrialist-with-the-midas-touch/1/391914.html

Sindhu Bhattacharya, 'Mallya senior was everything his son is not: How a rash Vijay Mallya jettisoned his father's principles', FirstPost.com, 10 March 2016, http://www.firstpost.com/business/

mallya-senior-was-everything-his-son-is-not-how-a-rash-vijay-mallya-jettisoned-his-fathers-principles-2667566.html

Mihir Dalal and P.R. Sanjai, 'How Vijay Mallya inherited an empire and proceeded to lose it', *Mint*, 27 February 2016, http://www.livemint.com/Companies/1YrLuntaxmNyeNoYFbUX1L/How-Vijay-Mallya-inherited-an-empire-and-then-proceeded-to-l.html

Chander Uday Singh, 'Vittal Mallya: Passing on', *India Today*, 15 November 1983, http://indiatoday.intoday.in/story/industrialist-vittal-mallya-dies-of-heart-attack-son-vijay-steps-in/1/372131.html

4. The Initial Years

Sindhu Bhattacharya, 'Mallya senior was everything his son is not: How a rash Vijay Mallya jettisoned his father's principles', FirstPost.com, 10 March 2016, http://www.firstpost.com/business/mallya-senior-was-everything-his-son-is-not-how-a-rash-vijay-mallya-jettisoned-his-fathers-principles-2667566.html

7. The Conquest of Shaw Wallace

Malini Bhupta, 'A new high', *India Today*, 11 April 2005, http://indiatoday.intoday.in/story/vijay-mallya-become-world-second-biggest-liquor-baron/1/194228.html

K. Giriprakash, 'S.P. Acharya: Liquor industry's original king', *Hindu Business Line*, 11 November 2015, http://www.thehindubusinessline.com/companies/sp-acharya-liquor-industrys-original-king/article7866918.ece

Sucheta Dalal, 'Manu Chhabria: A fierce fighter till the end', Rediff.com, 8 April 2002, http://www.rediff.com/money/2002/apr/08dalal.htm

Bhupesh Bhandari and Parul Gupta, 'Another Battle of the Bottle', *Business Standard*, 14 December 2002, http://www.business-standard.com/article/beyond-business/another-battle-of-the-bottle-102121401039_1.html

Vijay Kumar Kaushal, *Corporate Takeovers in India* (Sarup & Sons, 1995).

The Portfolio Book of Great Indian Business Stories: Riveting Tales of Business Leaders and Their Times (New Delhi: Penguin, 2015).
K. Giriprakash, *The Vijay Mallya Story* (New Delhi: Penguin, 2014).

8. Mallya's Foray into Politics

'Business tycoon Vijay Mallya joins JD-U', Rediff.com, 10 August 2002, http://www.rediff.com/news/2002/aug/10mallya.htm

Fakir Chand, 'Mallya's race to Rajya Sabha fizzles out', Rediff.com, 29 March 2000, http://www.rediff.com/news/2000/mar/29mallya.htm

'Vijay Mallya joins Janata Party', Rediff.com, 14 April 2003, http://www.rediff.com/news/2003/apr/14mallya1.htm

'Baron buys history', *India Today*, 19 April 2004, http://indiatoday.intoday.in/story/vijay-mallya-buys-tipu-sultans-legendary-sword/1/197209.html

Srinivasa Prasad, 'Here's why Mallya flopped: He used corporate strategies in politics, in business he used political ploys', FirstPost.com, 15 March 2016, http://www.firstpost.com/business/a-peek-inside-vijay-mallyas-mind-billionaire-who-dreamt-of-being-cm-and-boasted-he-could-buy-any-journo-in-india-2676036.html

PTI, 'Vijay Mallya buys Gandhi's items for $1.8m', *Times of India*, 6 March 2009, http://timesofindia.indiatimes.com/india/Vijay-Mallya-buys-Gandhis-items-for-1-8m/articleshow/4231248.cms

Suhrid Chattopadhyay, 'Mallya Picks Bulk Holding In Asian Age, Calcutta', *Business Standard*, 9 March 1998, http://www.business-standard.com/article/specials/mallya-picks-bulk-holding-in-asian-age-calcutta-198030901018_1.html

Ravi Sharma, 'Money Rules', *Frontline*, 4-17 December 2010, http://www.frontline.in/static/html/fl2725/stories/20101217272502400.htm

T.J.S. George, *Askew: A Short Biography of Bangalore* (New Delhi: Aleph Book Company, 2016).

'The lobbies that matter in Karnataka', Rediff.com, 30 April 2008, http://www.rediff.com/news/2008/apr/30spec.htm

IANS, 'Billionaire Vijay Mallya didn't hesitate to claim Rs 20,000 in perks as Rajya Sabha MP!', *Economic Times*, 22 April 2016,

http://economictimes.indiatimes.com/news/politics-and-nation/
billionaire-vijay-mallya-didnt-hesitate-to-claim-rs-20000-in-perks-
as-rajya-sabha-mp/articleshow/51941518.cms

9. Sporting Ventures

'Mukesh Ambani, Mallya, SRK win IPL bids', Rediff.com, 24 January
2008, http://www.rediff.com/money/2008/jan/24ipl1.htm
Tasmayee Laha Roy, 'Vijay Mallya's financial mess casts shadow over
Mohun Bagan and East Bengal', *Economic Times*, 9 April 2016,
http://economictimes.indiatimes.com/news/sports/vijay-mallyas-
financial-mess-casts-shadow-over-mohun-bagan-and-east-bengal/
articleshow/51749847.cms

10. Riding the Real Estate Boom

'Vijay Mallya's overseas properties include Trump Plaza condo',
Mint, 10 March 2016, http://www.livemint.com/Companies/6tC4
bSvsr7EoudIPFEk8GJ/Trump-Plaza-Condo-among-Vijay-Mallyas-
overseas-properties.html
Madhurima Nandy and Sharan Poovanna, 'Vijay Mallya's $20 million
'sky mansion' in Bengaluru is almost ready. But will he get to live
in it?' *Mint*, 20 March 2017, http://www.livemint.com/Compani
es/65IM1NYBFFgqWAF2osxIUO/Vijay-Mallyas-20-million-sky-
mansion-is-almost-ready-B.html
Madhurima Nandy and Sharan Poovanna, 'Homes in Kingfisher Towers
to be handed over to buyers this year', *Mint*, 18 May 2016, http://
www.livemint.com/Companies/bmCmCZhaeej54fUQD5LnkI/
Homes-in-Kingfisher-Towers-to-be-handed-over-to-buyers-this.
html
Anshul Dhamija, 'Vijay Mallya's white house in the sky', *Times of
India*, 18 October 2011, http://timesofindia.indiatimes.com/india/
Vijay-Mallyas-white-house-in-the-sky/articleshow/10397262.cms
Raghuvir Badrinath, 'Karnataka HC stops sale of flats at Mallya's
luxury Kingfisher Towers', *Business Standard*, 18 August
2014, http://www.business-standard.com/article/companies/

karnataka-hc-stops-sale-of-flats-at-mallya-s-luxury-kingfisher-towers-114081800002_1.html

11. The King of Good Times

Simi Garewal's interview with Vijay Mallya as part of her show 'Rendezvous with Simi Garewal' on 20 April 1999, https://www.youtube.com/watch?v=wAzcmeIjNsw

'Check out! Vijay Mallya's new girlfriend', *Mumbai Mirror*, 27 May 2013, http://mumbaimirror.indiatimes.com/columns/the-informer//articleshow/20288301.cms

12. The Bankers' Bane

Khushboo Narayan, 'Vijay Mallya actively participated in money laundering: ED tells court in complaint', *Indian Express*, 15 June 2017, http://indianexpress.com/article/business/companies/vijay-mallya-actively-participated-in-money-laundering-ed-informs-court-in-complaint-4704634/

PTI, 'Vijay Mallya created 20 shell companies, made personal staff directors: ED charge sheet', *Times of India*, 15 June 2017, http://timesofindia.indiatimes.com/india/vijay-mallya-created-20-shell-companies-made-personal-staff-directors-ed-chargesheet/articleshow/59165130.cms

ET Bureau, 'CBI arrests former IDBI chairman Yogesh Aggarwal and 8 others in Vijay Mallya loan default case', *Economic Times*, 24 January 2017, http://economictimes.indiatimes.com/news/politics-and-nation/cbi-arrests-former-idbi-chairman-yogesh-aggarwal-and-8-others-in-vijay-mallya-loan-default-case-sources/articleshow/56740233.cms

Virendrasingh Ghunawat, 'CBI arrests ex-IDBI Bank boss for Rs 900cr loan to Vijay Mallya's Kingfisher Airlines', *India Today*, 24 January 2017, http://indiatoday.intoday.in/story/vijay-mallya-kfa-idbi-bank-cbi-arrests/1/865012.html

Abhishek Sharan, 'Was IDBI ex-CMD behind Rs 900-cr loan to Vijay Mallya's airlines?', *Hindustan Times*, 12 March 2016, http://

www.hindustantimes.com/business/mallya-row-idbi-chief-may-have-played-key-role-in-sanctioning-kfa-rs-900-cr-loan/story-pEvmwVWmx0psCqLnixzsdK.html

PTI, 'Holiday meeting helped Mallya get IDBI Bank loan', *Hindu Business Line*, 29 January 2017, http://www.thehindubusinessline.com/money-and-banking/mallyabank-cmd-holiday-meeting-led-to-hasty-sanction-of-rs-350-cr-loan-ed/article9508209.ece

Khushboo Narayan, Johnson T.A. and Shaji Vikraman, 'From bang to bust: The Kingfisher story', *Indian Express*, 14 March 2016, http://indianexpress.com/article/india/india-news-india/sunday-story-once-upon-a-time-there-was-a-king-vijay-mallya/

TNN, 'SBI had offered to settle KFA loan issue with Vijay Mallya', *Times of India*, 4 July 2016, http://timesofindia.indiatimes.com/business/india-business/SBI-had-offered-to-settle-KFA-loan-issue-with-Vijay-Mallya/articleshow/53037842.cms

Krishnadas Rajagopal, 'Contempt notice issued to Mallya after banks unable to locate his wealth', *Hindu*, 25 July 2016, http://www.thehindu.com/news/national/Contempt-notice-issued-to-Mallya-after-banks-unable-to-locate-his-wealth/article14508005.ece

Mayur Shetty, 'Vijay Mallya's Kingfisher Villa on the block for Rs 85 crore', *Times of India*, 13 September 2016, http://timesofindia.indiatimes.com/business/india-business/Vijay-Mallyas-Kingfisher-Villa-on-the-block-for-Rs-85-crore/articleshow/54306600.cms

TNN, 'Lenders get Kingfisher equity at 60% premium', *Times of India*, 7 April 2011, http://timesofindia.indiatimes.com/business/india-business/Lenders-get-Kingfisher-equity-at-60-premium/articleshow/7894180.cms

13. The Mallya Empire Falls Apart

P.R. Sanjai, 'Vijay Mallya quits as United Spirits chairman', *Mint*, 26 February 2016, http://www.livemint.com/Companies/Pb0AtrvY5KrZua4CdNnKHJ/Vijay-Mallya-quits-as-chairman-of-United-Spirits.html

Saloni Shukla, 'Vijay Mallya's lenders eye Diageo's $75 million severance payment', *Economic Times*, 27 February 2016, http://

economictimes.indiatimes.com/industry/cons-products/liquor/vijay-mallyas-lenders-eye-diageos-75-million-severance-payment/articleshow/51162363.cms

Amy Kazmin, 'Diageo pays $75m to Vijay Mallya to step down from United Spirits', *Financial Times*, 26 February 2016, https://www.ft.com/content/819cb09c-dbe0-11e5-9ba8-3abc1e7247e4

Uttara Choudhury, 'Vijay Mallya's famed US beer maker Mendocino in trouble too', FirstPost.com, 23 May 2016, http://www.firstpost.com/business/vijay-mallyas-famed-us-beer-maker-mendocino-in-trouble-too-2793984.html

HT Correspondent, 'Vijay Mallya finds 75 million reasons to resign as USL chairman, *Hindustan Times*, 26 February 2016, http://www.hindustantimes.com/business/vijay-mallya-resigns-as-united-spirits-chairman-will-move-to-uk/story-0aosxQQttTwdj9REKP0AIL.html

Index